# A Way of Giving

# Sam Greenbank

Visit us online at www.authorsonline.co.uk

A Bright Pen Book

Text Copyright © Sam Greenbank 2011

Cover design by © Adrian Mallett

All rights reserved. No part of this publication may be reproduced, stored in a retrieval system, or transmitted in any form or by any means, electronic, mechanical, photocopy, recording or otherwise, without prior written permission of the copyright owner. Nor can it be circulated in any form of binding or cover other than that in which it is published and without similar condition including this condition being imposed on a subsequent purchaser.

Scripture quotations taken from the HOLY BIBLE, NEW INTERNATIONAL VERSION, Copyright © 1973, 1978, 1984 by International Bible Society. Used by permission.

Some scriptures and additional materials quoted are from the *Good News Bible* © 1994 published by the Bible Societies/HarperCollins Publishers Ltd UK, *Good News Bible* © American Bible Society 1966, 1971, 1976, 1992. Used with permission.

British Library Cataloguing Publication Data.
A catalogue record for this book is available from the British Library

ISBN 9780755214136

Authors OnLine Ltd
19 The Cinques
Gamlingay, Sandy
Bedfordshire SG19 3NU
England

This book is also available in e-book format, details of which are available at www.authorsonline.co.uk

# CONTENTS

Preface.

| | | |
|---|---|---|
| Chapter 1. | Jesus Came for the Poor | Luke 4: v. 16–21 |
| Chapter 2. | Second-Class Citizens | Mark 2: v. 14–17 |
| Chapter 3. | Look Up | Luke 18: v. 9–14 |
| Chapter 4. | Poor and Happy? | Matthew 5: v. 3 and Luke 6: v.20 |
| Chapter 5. | Samaritans | Luke 10: v. 25–35 |
| Chapter 6. | Gifts That Count | Mark 12: v. 41–44 (GNB) |
| Chapter 7. | Where's Your Heart? | Matthew 6: v. 21 (GNB) |
| Chapter 8. | Going for Gold? | Matthew 6: v. 24 |
| Chapter 9. | Making It Big | Luke 12: v. 16–21 |
| Chapter 10. | Death to Me | Matthew 16: v. 24 |
| Chapter 11. | Worlds Apart | Matthew 16: v. 25–26 |
| Chapter 12. | Weeds | Matthew 13: v. 3–9 and v. 22 |

| | | |
|---|---|---|
| Chapter 13. | Spring into Life | John 12: v. 23–26 |
| Chapter 14. | Too Much to Ask | Matthew 19: v. 16–22 |
| Chapter 15. | Zacchaeus | Luke 19: v. 1–10 |
| Chapter 16. | The Loophole | Matthew 19: v. 23–26 |
| Chapter 17. | Asking the Impossible? | Luke 14: v. 33 |
| Chapter 18. | Top Priority | Matthew 13: v. 44–46 |
| Chapter 19. | The Alternative | Matthew 6: v. 25–34 |
| Chapter 20. | The Main Job | Mark 1: v. 16–20 |
| Chapter 21. | Travelling Light | Luke 9: v. 1–3 |
| Chapter 22. | Nest Egg | Matthew 6: v. 19–21 |
| Chapter 23. | Loan Repayment | Luke 6: v. 35 |
| Chapter 24. | Ours to Share | Luke 6: v. 24 |
| Chapter 25. | God's Entrepreneur | Matthew 25: v. 14–30 |
| Chapter 26. | Do-gooders | Matthew 25: v. 31–40 |
| Chapter 27. | The Great Reversal | Matthew 20: v. 16 |
| Chapter 28. | The Rich Man and Lazarus | Luke 16: v. 19–31 |
| Epilogue | | John 12: v. 6 and Matthew 7: v. 24 |

# Preface

This short, easy-to-read book is a commentary on what Jesus had to say about wealth and possessions. It started out as a question – or rather a problem. I knew that Jesus came for the poor in particular and many of his stories and teachings were about the dangers of being wealthy. Yet the reality seems to contradict this – large and successful churches are found in leafy suburbs full of educated, middle-class people, whereas churches in poorer districts are struggling to survive. I know this, having lived for a few years on a Birmingham Council overspill estate and, later, in a much more affluent area.

I was also keenly aware that our faith has little obvious relevance to those who don't already share it. It doesn't impinge on the daily life of the believer, as far as anyone else can see. Worse, there seemed to be a pretence or hypocrisy about it, though I couldn't identify my misgivings. I believe that Jesus was intensely practical and that he wanted everybody to be his disciple, which means that our form of discipleship must be accessible to all.

A Baptist minister once said to me that the Church had never had the proletariat – it had always been middle class. I couldn't argue with him because he was a scholar whose learning I respected, but my own feeling was: why? So I began to read. I read the gospels several times, looking for all the references to wealth and possessions – whether in direct teaching, conversations or events – trying to see the relevance of each passage to our lives in the twenty-first century. You can do it for yourself. It took me years to read it all and think it through, but you might do it in a few weeks or months. I didn't find an answer to the question that prompted my search – that slipped away into irrelevance – but what I learned changed my life, my faith, my foundations.

This book is the product of my study. I hope you enjoy it. There are 28 chapters, each based on a separate teaching, story or event. A chapter consists of a passage from one of the gospels and a comment on its relevance to the modern disciple.

You can dash through it all in an hour or so, if you choose, but better to take it slowly, mull each passage over, enjoy the pictures and see how well your own lifestyle and thinking chime with what Jesus had to say.

Love is the basic human need and the good news of the Christian gospel is that God loves us despite ourselves. I have lots of friends who love me, a loving family and best of all a loving wife who has supported me for our many years together.

Several friends have contributed to the book – David Hawkins, my friend of many years, many walks and many debates has spent long hours editing the text both for content and grammar. Kenneth Breare (FRPS), an old friend from Mirfield days has supplied the infra-red images, Adrian Mallett the modern art for the cover and other pictures and Alan Gilliam the photographs.

Your friend in the exciting adventure of following Jesus,

Sam Greenbank

# 1. Jesus Came for the Poor

He went to Nazareth, where he had been brought up, and on the Sabbath day he went into the synagogue, as was his custom. And he stood up to read. The scroll of the prophet Isaiah was handed to him. Unrolling it, he found the place where it is written:
"The Spirit of the Lord is on me,
because he has anointed me
to preach good news to the poor..."
Then he rolled up the scroll, gave it back to the attendant and sat down. The eyes of everyone in the synagogue were fastened on him, and he began by saying to them, "Today this scripture is fulfilled in your hearing."
(Luke 4: v. 16–21)

This was a brave and bold thing to do. Jesus had just started his ministry and news about him was getting around so he went back to his home town to face the folk who knew him best. He was letting them know who he was – the promised Messiah, the fulfilment of the old scriptures; what his mission was – to bring good news; and who his target audience were – the poor.

Jesus refers to the poor many times, but who were they? It was such a long time ago, not to mention a different culture and country, that his meaning of the word 'poor' was surely very different from ours. Were they the crowds of ordinary folk who flocked to hear his teaching and see his miracles of healing? Or were they like those who today sleep in shop doorways, or even the Third World poor who grow thin and weak with hunger?

We don't know for sure, but it's not difficult to draw a poverty line which runs through any age and culture and it's not difficult to decide which side of it you are on. If, for instance, you haven't enough money for any sort of luxury except those which come your way by chance, if you can't afford a proper diet or can't keep warm in winter, or if you've no place to call home – then you're poor by any standards. It is easy to think, in the comfort of our homes, that people this poor don't exist in our country today but they do. Jesus came for them.

Then there are those who are poor in power and influence – the ordinary folk, the masses. They might have enough to live on and they certainly have the vote which people didn't have in Jesus' day, but they don't feel they count for much. They are the poorly paid or unemployed; they are easily tempted into debt; they didn't get much out of their education and they don't expect much for their kids; their hope is in the football pools or the lottery; nobody wants their opinion but everybody wants their money. There are lots of these people today and there were probably many in Jesus' day. Jesus came for them.

It would be wrong to say that Jesus ignored the rich. Many of his disciples were either in business or had good jobs. Perhaps they weren't rich but they weren't poor either. Matthew was a tax collector and the brothers Peter and Andrew, and James and John had at least a share in fishing businesses. So how could they be not only part of the target audience but at the very centre of his mission? Perhaps it was because they had left everything to follow Jesus (Matthew 19: v. 27). They might have decided that Jesus was the treasure they were looking for, so anything which stood in the way had to go.

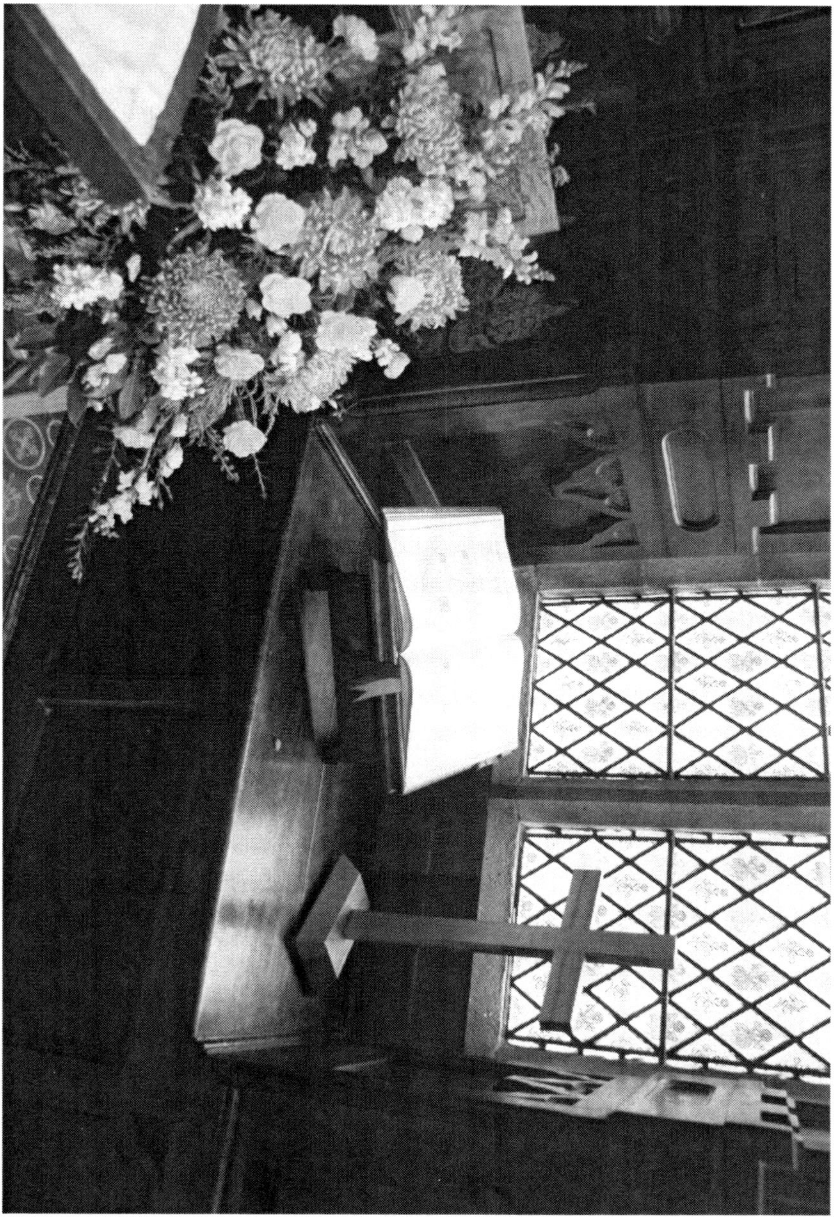

## 2. Second-Class Citizens

As he walked along, he saw Levi son of Alphaeus sitting at the tax collector's booth. "Follow me," Jesus told him, and Levi got up and followed him.

While Jesus was having dinner at Levi's house, many tax collectors and "sinners" were eating with him and his disciples, for there were many who followed him. When the teachers of the law who were Pharisees saw him eating with the "sinners" and tax collectors, they asked his disciples: "Why does he eat with tax collectors and 'sinners'?"

On hearing this, Jesus said to them, "It is not the healthy who need a doctor, but the sick. I have not come to call the righteous, but sinners."

(Mark 2: v. 14–17)

Here's another slant on the situation. You couldn't say that tax collectors were poor. We know that at least some of them were well off. The tax collection system allowed them to cheat so they cheated and paid the price in social isolation. Worse, they collected taxes for the occupying Romans and so were seen as collaborators with the enemy. They were hated, beyond the pale – outcasts. They were at the bottom of their social pile. No one invited them for tea except another tax collector. Jesus came for them.

Tax collectors were not the only kind of second-class citizen in Palestine at that time. Samaritans were mocked and despised for their ancestry. There were the hated Romans occupying the land as well as Greeks from an earlier occupation. Lepers were excluded, women didn't count for much and then there were the slaves. Jesus trampled on these prejudices. He seemed to go out of his way to welcome people from these groups, to the great annoyance of his enemies and, probably, the discomfort of his friends.

Fortunately, we don't have their kind of tax collectors but we do have a class system and powerful and insidious ways of excluding the sort of people we don't want. The dividing lines of our society can be found in many of our institutions and social activities whether it is in schools, sports, shopping, pubs, restaurants, hotels, churches or housing. Some institutions seem to target or attract particular social groups – restaurants for the middle class, cafés for the working class. The lines are often financial but not necessarily so. They can result from a sense of inferiority or a fear of embarrassment.

My wife and I had a first-hand experience of these dividing lines when we took a friend of ours, who lives on a large council estate, into a hotel for an afternoon coffee. She was amused, excited, frightened of making a mistake and a little uncomfortable. It wasn't expensive but she would never have ventured into the hotel on her own.

Perhaps it is unfair to compare the social prejudices in a land under occupation two thousand years ago with our own in peace time but it is clear that, whatever such prejudices were and however they arose, Jesus would have nothing to do with them except to attack them. Each person was of infinite value to Jesus and he expected his followers to be of the same mind.

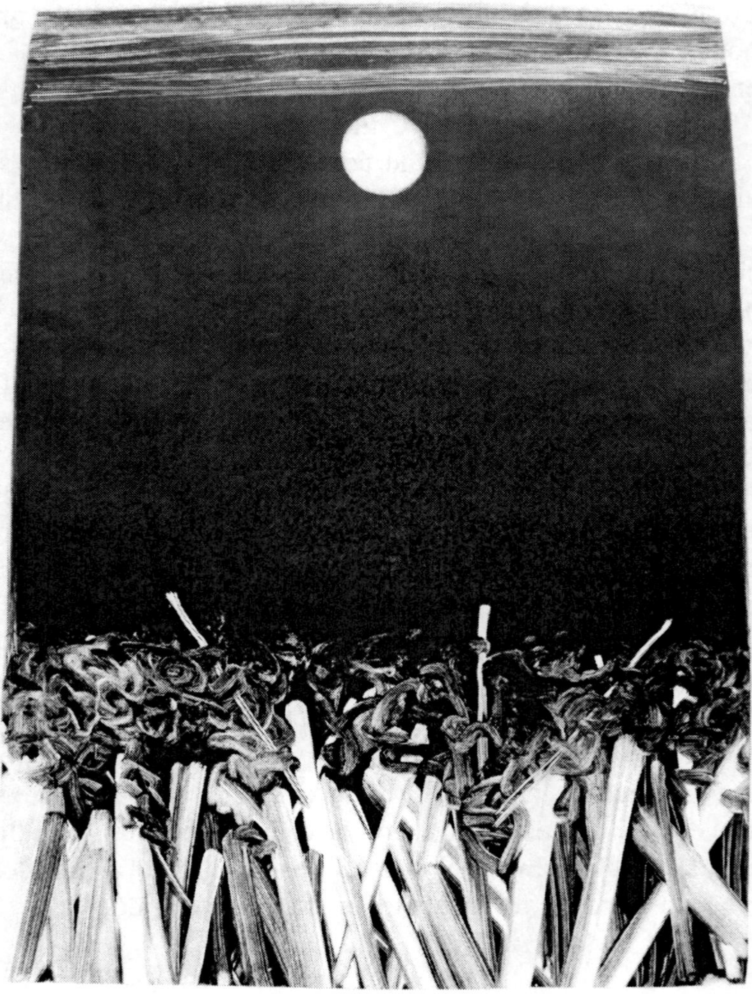

# 3. Look Up

To some who were confident of their own righteousness and looked down on everybody else, Jesus told this parable: "Two men went to the temple to pray – one a Pharisee and the other a tax collector. The Pharisee stood up and prayed about himself: 'God, I thank you that I am not like all other men – robbers, evildoers, adulterers – or even like this tax collector. I fast twice a week and give a tenth of all I get.'

"But the tax collector stood at a distance. He would not even look up to heaven, but beat his breast and said, 'God have mercy on me, a sinner.'

"I tell you that this man, rather than the other, went home justified before God. For everyone who exalts himself will be humbled, and he who humbles himself will be exalted."

(Luke 18: v. 9–14)

Here's a reason, in picture language, why Jesus came for the poor and the outcast. Only those who are at the bottom can look up and take a childlike delight in the sense of forgiveness and the chance of a new start which God offers.

Those who are at the top don't need a new start – they have made it already. So they tend to look down on the rest, blaming them for their lack of success and even accusing them of fecklessness, immorality and lack of class. It's extremely difficult for a successful person to retain a true humility because success means being stroked by an admiring public and we can't help purring.

So we miss the blessing because we fail to look up. We don't recognize that we are really in the same boat as that miserable lot over there. We allow what's really a bit of luck, of birth or brains or chance, to fix the direction of our gaze downwards – the ultimate folly?

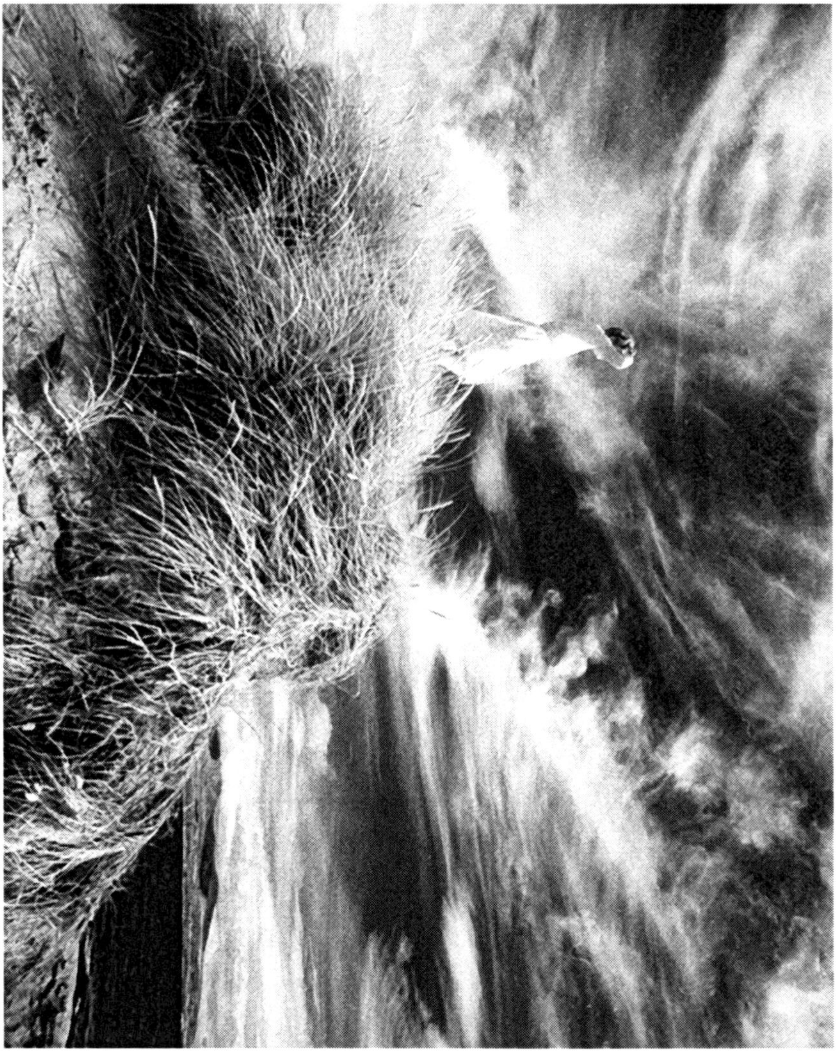

# 4. Poor and Happy?

"Blessed are the poor in spirit, for theirs is the kingdom of heaven."
(Matthew 5: v. 3)

"Blessed are you who are poor, for yours is the kingdom of God."
(Luke 6: v. 20)

Clearly, these are two versions of what Jesus said. The second one is hard to swallow unless you happen to be poor but the first gives us a way out. Luke always seems to take the harder line when recording the teaching of Jesus on wealth and possessions. Perhaps he had given up everything to follow Jesus when he joined Paul on the great missionary journeys recorded in Acts and was, therefore, more inclined towards the financial demands which Jesus makes.

Why does Jesus say that the poor are blessed? (Some modern translations use the word 'happy'.) Surely he can't mean that poverty is a happy state of affairs? Many good people spend their lives fighting it and good governments do the same. The trouble is that as soon as we have a bit of money we are into spending or saving or both, and it is a drug which both stimulates and binds us. We used to depend on God, our family and our friends, but now we've got pension schemes, investments, insurance policies, a nest egg in the building society, a house of our own etc.

But Jesus says it is a bad swap. The poor don't have any of

these things. They have to look outward to friends and family and upward to God. It may be that the kind of happiness they enjoy is far better than anything that wealth has to offer.

Then there is the way out. Perhaps we can be 'poor in spirit' without being poor in fact. If so, we might be able to keep our wealth and possessions intact and still have the blessing.

Because it's not quite clear what Jesus meant by 'poor in spirit', it is ever so easy to invent an interpretation to suit our own circumstances. For instance, we might think our generous giving to charities or the Church shows that we are not dependent on our wealth. Or we might do voluntary work with some disadvantaged group and hope that will do.

Whatever our interpretation, it seems certain that the 'poor in spirit' are the givers who hold their wealth and possessions with a very light grip and never have to look for a needy cause. It is difficult to imagine any such person becoming well off at all because their wealth is scattered along the way and never has the chance to accumulate.

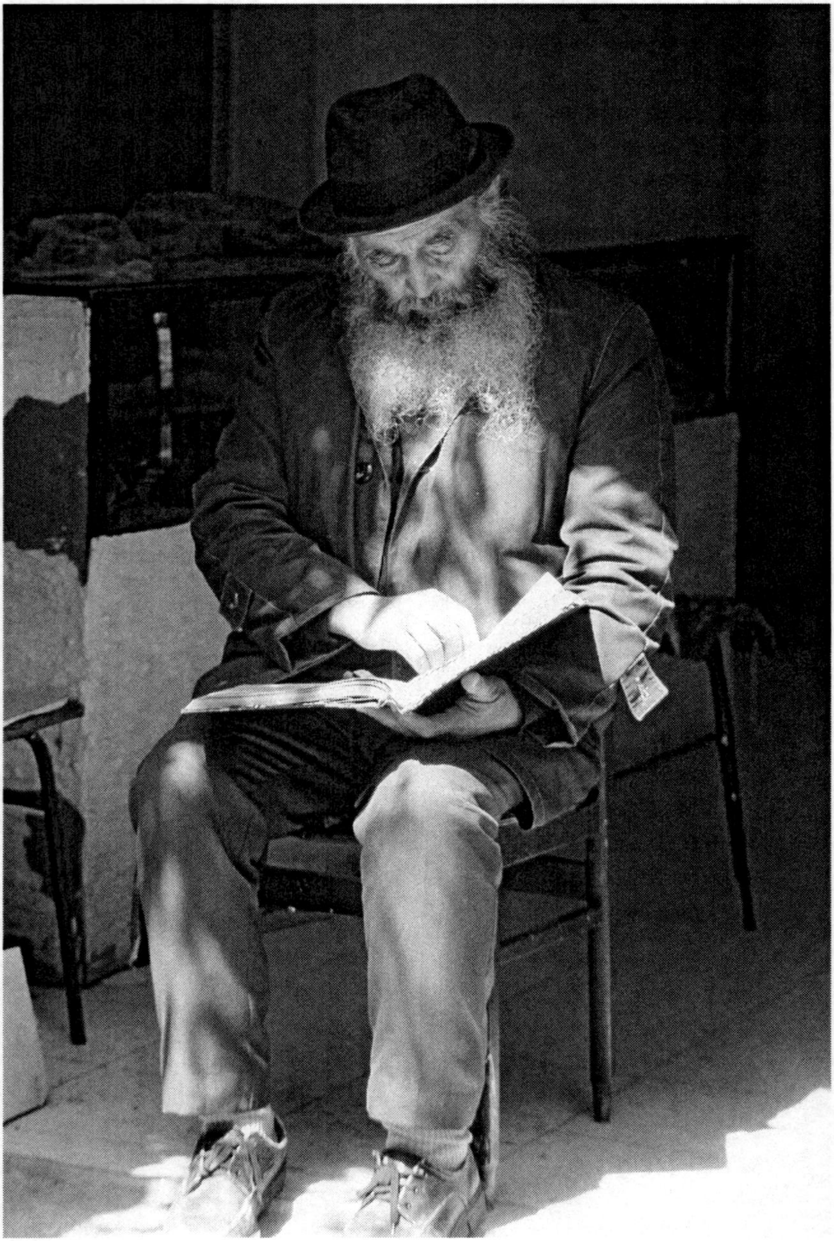

# 5. Samaritans

An expert in the law stood up to test Jesus. "Teacher," he asked, "what must I do to inherit eternal life?"

"What is written in the Law?" he replied. "How do you read it?"

He answered: "'Love the Lord your God with all your heart and with all your soul and with all your strength and with all your mind'; and, 'Love your neighbour as yourself.'"

"You have answered correctly," Jesus replied. "Do this and you will live."

But he wanted to justify himself, so he asked Jesus, "And who is my neighbour?"

In reply Jesus said: "A man was going down from Jerusalem to Jericho, when he fell into the hands of robbers. They stripped him of his clothes, beat him and went away, leaving him half dead. A priest happened to be going down the same road, and when he saw the man, he passed by on the other side. So too, a Levite, when he came to the place and saw him, passed by on the other side. But a Samaritan, as he travelled, came where the man was; and when he saw him, he took pity on him. He went to him and bandaged his wounds, pouring on oil and wine. Then he put the man on his own donkey, brought him to an inn and took care of him. The next day he took out two silver coins and gave them to the innkeeper. 'Look after him,' he said, 'and when I return, I will reimburse you for any extra expense you may have.'"

(Luke 10: v. 25–35)

This is a tremendous story. The main plot is about living out our response to the love of God in a practical way. In the minor plot Jesus teases the expert who questioned him, by giving the star role in the story to the despised Samaritan and by casting the Levite in a bad light as one who didn't stop to help the wounded man.

Surely Jesus didn't cast the Levite in a bad light just to wound the lawyer who asked the question but because things often do happen that way Rich and important people are usually far too busy to disrupt their day for every unfortunate person who appeals to them for help – they would never get anything done.

On the other hand, those who are less embroiled in the affairs of the world will drop what they are doing in order to meet another person's need because the other person is more important to them.

It's not always true of course. Here are two recent events, the first to show how good the busy public can be in response to someone's distress and the second to confirm the point Jesus was making in the story.

I was travelling on the London underground with my wife and an elderly friend. We had to use the escalator to climb up from one level to the next. It was a long and steep escalator and our friend failed to get a firm footing. I was behind her and she fell backwards onto me. I could not stop her falling and we both tumbled downwards. I damaged my hand but she split her head in two places and blood flowed from the wounds onto her clothes and shoulders. I managed to stop the escalator and then two wonderful things happened: everyone stood still – no one tried to pass us – and then two suited gentlemen picked her up, carried her to the top and stayed with her until first aid arrived.

The second story concerns five lads who shared a house in a Northern university city. One of them was from a very wealthy family, while another was relatively poor. It was the rich boy's 21$^{st}$ birthday and his four friends were all invited to the posh do at father's Knightsbridge mansion.

They borrowed or hired some evening wear, packed sleeping bags and everything needed for a night's stay into their old Mini and drove off to London for the exciting party.

Unfortunately, Father had hijacked the party as a business opportunity and it was peopled by the rich and famous. This was exciting in a way but when the party came to an end, the lads weren't allowed to unroll their sleeping bags as expected because, well, it wouldn't do – some of the important guests were staying the night. And so they were out on the street in the early hours with nowhere to go and in no fit state to get there.

Fortunately, the poor student had an uncle and aunt who lived in a terrace house in a down-market part of town not too far away. He hadn't seen them for years but he was sure they would put the four of them up. After much banging and calling, the door opened and they were warmly welcomed by Uncle and Aunt. Soon, drinks were flowing, cake tins were opened and every good thing in their cupboard was brought out. The lads finally made it to their sleeping bags and slept well and long.

The party continued next day with a five-star brunch, though they would have been happy with a piece of toast. They finally left with a sincere invitation to return.

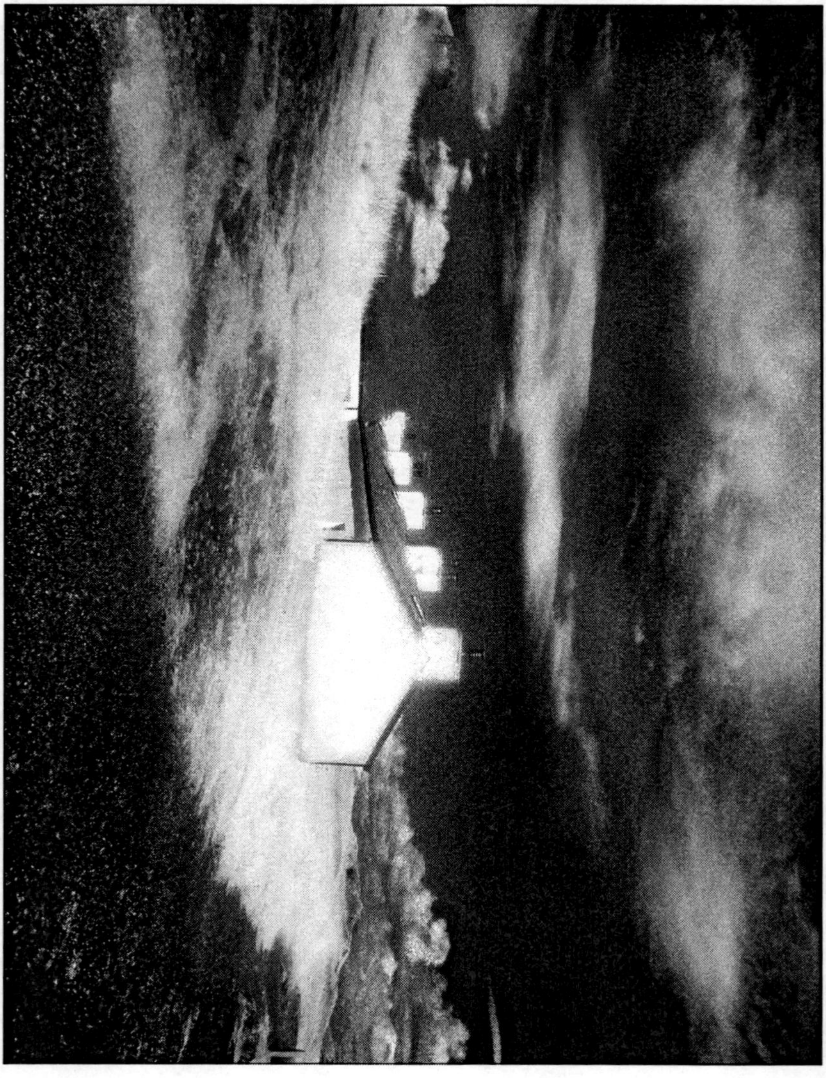

# 6. Gifts That Count

As Jesus sat near the temple treasury, he watched people as they dropped in their money. Many rich men dropped in a lot of money; then a poor widow came along and dropped in two small copper coins worth about a penny. He called his disciples together and said to them, "I tell you that this widow put more in the offering box than all the others. For the others put in what they had to spare of their riches but she, poor as she is, put in all she had – she gave all she had to live on."
(Mark 12: v. 41–44 (GNB))

This is a crazy thing for Jesus to say. The temple treasurer certainly wouldn't agree with him that the widow gave more than the others. What he wanted was lots of rich people who felt the need to make handsome donations. The widow's two coins wouldn't make a scrap of difference.

Yes, the widow did put more in relative to her income – she went home absolutely broke whereas the rich men's gifts didn't cause a flicker in their bank accounts. When they got back home they would carry on exactly as before. (Things haven't changed, the poor still give away more in proportion to their income than the rich.)

The widow gave more in real terms because she gave herself with her gift – her energies, her prayers, her hopes, her body and soul. Her heart was with her gift. The hearts of the rich men were with the money they kept back at home. Their ample gifts were designed to reinforce the status quo and their own self-esteem but in the widow's gift were all her longings for justice and goodness.

The world is full of rich people who are wanting to look good and their gifts are very welcome but they won't change anything. Revolutions start at the bottom.

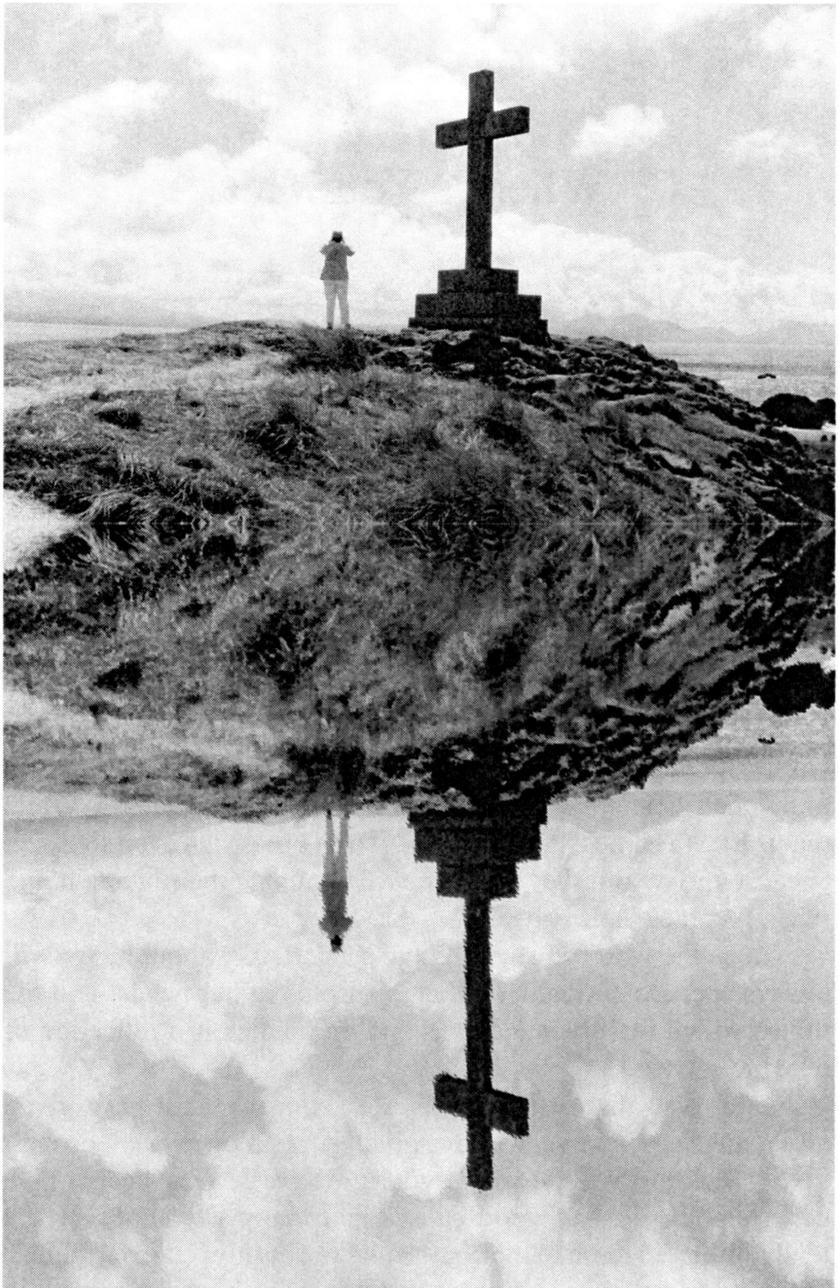

# 7. Where's Your Heart?

"Your heart will always be where your riches are."
(Matthew 6: v. 21 (GNB))

This simple statement by Jesus is a fact of life. It has been plucked out of its context here but that does not detract from its meaning or diminish its power because it has universal application and can, therefore, stand alone. (A fuller quotation is the subject of Chapter 22.)

You might say that it doesn't apply to the majority of the world's population, because they don't have any riches on which to set their hearts but spend all their energies on survival. While that is true to some extent, there is a strong message even for them because the wealth they long for will captivate their hearts if and when it comes their way.

Notice the word 'always'. There's a certainty about it. We will always spend our wealth – what is surplus to our needs – on the things which really matter to us and our choice is a reflection of our true selves.

Notice also that the saying is not about what we have given away, unless, of course, we have given everything away. It doesn't say, 'your heart will be where your gifts are'. Many people give generously to lots of good causes and many Christians give a tenth of their income to the church and to charities (the old 'tithe') but this little saying is bigger than that. It's about our wealth in cash or possessions – our 'treasure' which we have tried to build up over the years. It's that surplus which we have been able to save or spend on what we liked.

So where's your heart by this measure? Where's your money? Is it in the bank, your house, your car, the kids, your holidays, your pension fund? Or are you one of those lucky ones who don't really know because it has slipped through your fingers in a thousand kindnesses that never really counted.

The response of the righteous to the praise of the King in the judgement story in Matthew 25 is marvellous: they could not remember doing any kindnesses to him.

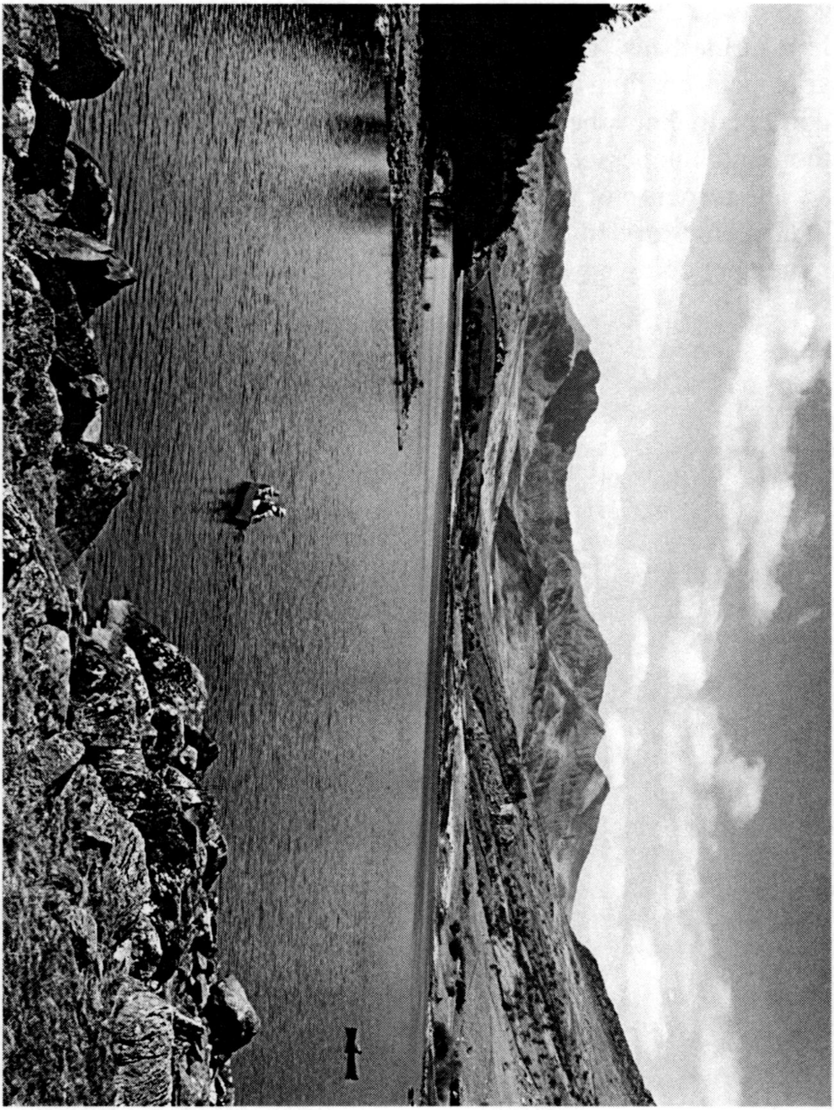

# 8. Going for Gold?

"You cannot serve both God and Money."
(Matthew 6: v. 24)

Jesus doesn't say that it is very difficult to serve both God and money, nor does he just warn us to watch out for the dangers. He simply says it can't be done.

However, you can tip-toe round it without much trouble by insisting that you don't 'serve' money really, whatever it might look like to other people. None of the well-to-do Christians in our large suburban churches would admit that money was their master. On the contrary, they would say their aim was firmly fixed on the Kingdom of God. They might also add that God always provides for those who trust him and if only you would think the same or, better still, join their number, you would enjoy the same benefits.

Before Jesus came, everybody thought like this. If you were faithful, God would reward you with long life, health and prosperity. There is great truth in it, of course. If you are at peace with God then you are at peace with yourself and others. You are more likely to be in good health and enjoy right relationships. Also, the nation which is honest, hard working, law abiding and cares for all its citizens will prosper. As the old saying puts it: 'righteousness makes a nation great' (Proverbs 14: v. 34). This truth hasn't changed but it is a collective truth which can't be hijacked by individual Christians for their own personal gain and comfort. Christians are no more immune to life's misfortunes than anyone else. As Jesus observed: "Your Father makes his sun to shine on bad and good people alike" (Matthew 5: v. 45).

The kingdom of God which Jesus ushered in has nothing whatsoever to do with personal gain. It is based on sacrificial giving. Jesus gave himself to the world in his life and by his death and he invites his followers to find their true life by giving themselves away to him. Their response can only be expressed in service to others. You can't give and love like he did while making a pile on the side.

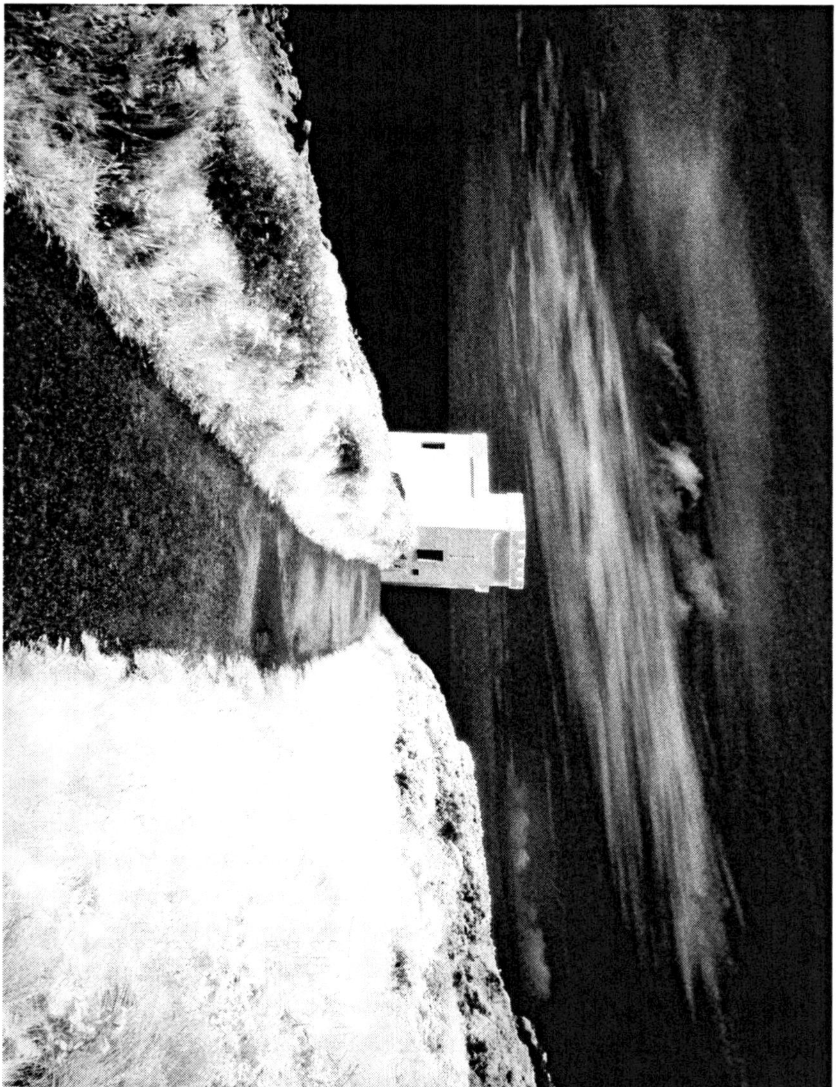

# 9. Making It Big

[Jesus] told them this parable: "The ground of a certain rich man produced a good crop. He thought to himself, 'What shall I do? I have no place to store my crops.'

"Then he said, 'This is what I'll do. I will tear down my barns and build bigger ones, and there I will store all my grain and my goods. And I'll say to myself, "You have plenty of good things laid up for many years. Take life easy; eat, drink and be merry."'

"But God said to him, 'You fool! This very night your life will be demanded from you. Then who will get what you have prepared for yourself?'

"This is how it will be with anyone who stores up things for himself but is not rich towards God."

(Luke 12: v. 16–21)

This is a success story, so why should Jesus spoil it? Here's a successful farmer who has worked hard all his life, cared well for his land, planted the right crops for the soil and the market, driven a hard but fair bargain and reaped the reward for his labours. This bumper crop is just a bonus – the icing on the cake – and it is big enough to persuade him to put his feet up. At last, he can sit back and enjoy a well-earned rest. Better still, he has enough stacked away to do all those things he's been dreaming about for years: that cottage by the sea; or perhaps a swimming pool; a new car – "why not, you deserve it" – or a world cruise. You name it, he can have it.

But Jesus calls him a "fool" for making the assumption that heaven is here and now and that we have the keys. He has forgotten that life has an end which is not of our choosing and when that time comes we shall be as naked as when we were born. He has spent his life building up for an experience which is short-lived, when he could have been building up for one that lasts forever.

Moreover, his barns full of grain will count against him when he meets his Maker because they are ample evidence that he had decided to be rich in things rather than rich towards God. He wasn't rich towards God because his life was focussed on himself – there is no mention at all of his wealth benefiting anyone else, not even his wife, and there's a humorous emphasis on 'I', 'me' and 'my' when he talks to himself in greedy delight about his plans for a future of ease and plenty.

There is no criticism of his success. Perhaps if his success had been directed towards someone else it would have been acceptable but that is a bit of a pipe dream. People do all sorts of heroic things for others but making a pile of money isn't one of them. Acquisitiveness is an incurable and terminal illness. If you are a giver, the pile doesn't start to grow because you don't have to look far for a needy cause and it gets scattered along the way.

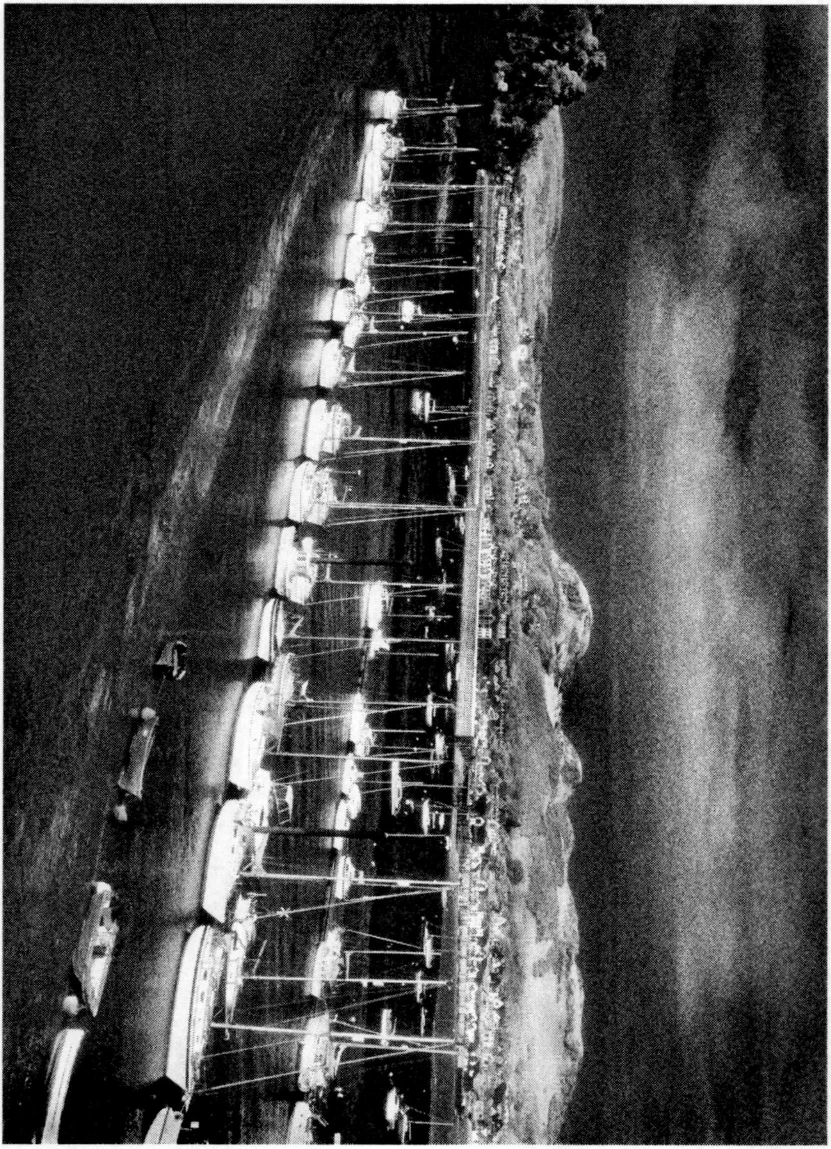

# 10. Death to Me

Jesus said to his disciples, "If anyone would come after me, he must deny himself and take up his cross and follow me."
(Matthew 16: v. 24)

In Palestine at the time of Jesus, crucifixion was the common form of execution and condemned criminals had to carry their own crosses to the place of execution just as Jesus himself had to do. So here Jesus is challenging his would-be followers to a kind of voluntary death. The self has to be denied and even put to death in order to follow him.

It sounds painful but what does it mean and is it really necessary? It all depends on how committed you are to promoting Number One. If you yourself are at the centre of all your efforts, dreams and ambitions, you are in for a hard time when you choose to follow Jesus because he wants to blow them all away and replace yourself with himself. On the other hand, if you are one of those lovely people who delight in promoting the interests, ambitions, opinions and even beliefs of others, then you will find it easy to follow Jesus because he will be the one you have been looking for.

This doesn't mean that Jesus wants an army of weak-minded people who have no energy or opinions of their own but he does want followers whose focus is outward and upward. Their individual energy is not lost by this but is tossed into the cauldron of the Church community which then boils up and over with an energy far exceeding the sum of the individual believers.

Is it necessary? The first of the Ten Commandments given by God to Moses is: 'You shall have no other gods before me'. Jesus didn't withdraw that commandment but focussed it upon himself. He is not asking us to stop living in order to follow him but to stop living for ourselves. If we are determined to keep our other gods, then it's no use trying to take Jesus on board because it won't work. He didn't give his life for us so that we could nod to him on Sundays.

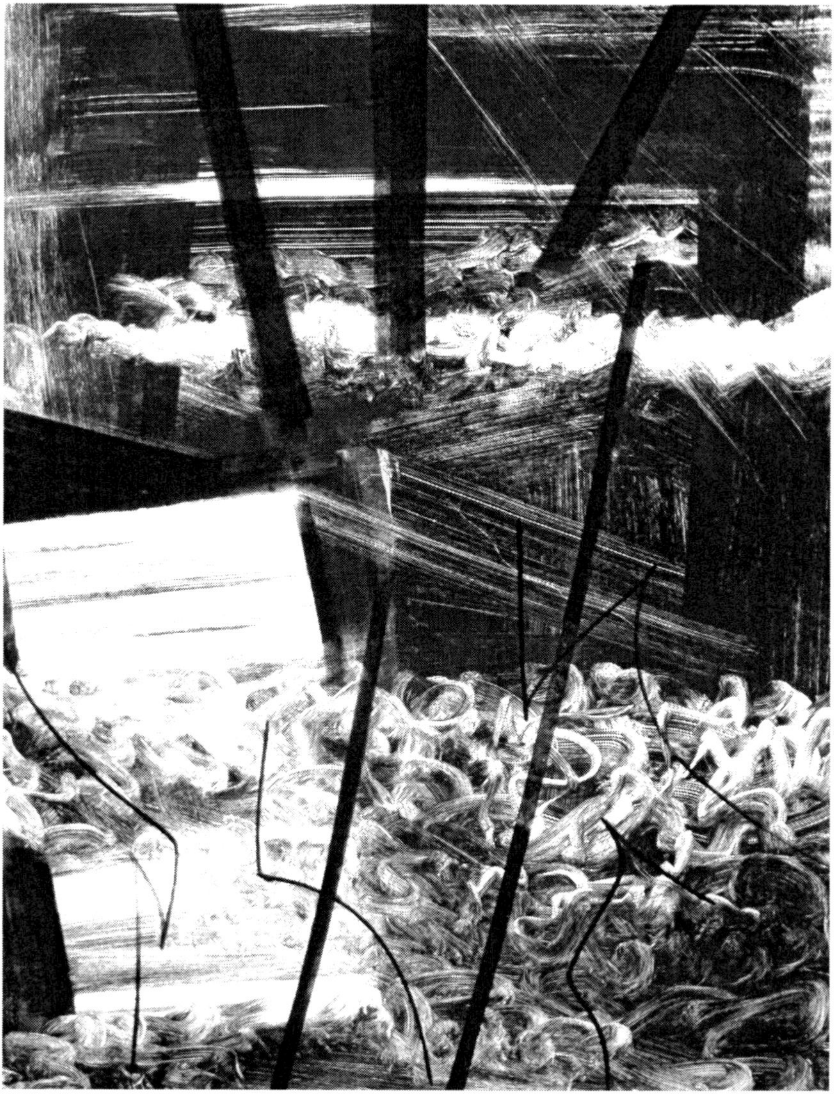

# 11. Worlds Apart

"Whoever wants to save his life will lose it, but whoever loses his life for me will find it. What good will it be for a man if he gains the whole world, yet forfeits his soul?"
                                        (Matthew 16: v. 25–26)

Jesus is such an extremist. With him, it's black or white; in or out; heaven or hell; life or death; total loss or total gain. Surely, there's a grey area for 'nice' Christians like me? We live by skilfully treading the middle ground but Jesus isn't there. He seems to inhabit the extremities, always demanding more and only promising the utmost to those who give everything.

It's easy to think, in our selfish world, that everyone just lives for themselves but it isn't true. Self-interest might be the basis of our economic system but a marriage won't last long on it and a sense of community can't be built on it either. Fortunately, there are many lovely people who give themselves away in favour of someone else or some worthy cause. They are not all in the Church and they are not just the meek and unsung either. Our history is full of unselfish heroes.

Jesus loves such people because they are willing to lose their own lives and he wants to claim them for his own: "If you will lose your life for me, you will find your true self," as another version puts it.

You can't give yourself away, like Jesus wants us to do, and feather your own nest at the same time. The Jesus way is about giving and the world's way is about getting and keeping. They are completely opposite ways of living and they don't meet in the middle. If you want the one, you have to ditch the other and there is no looking back to see what you have missed.

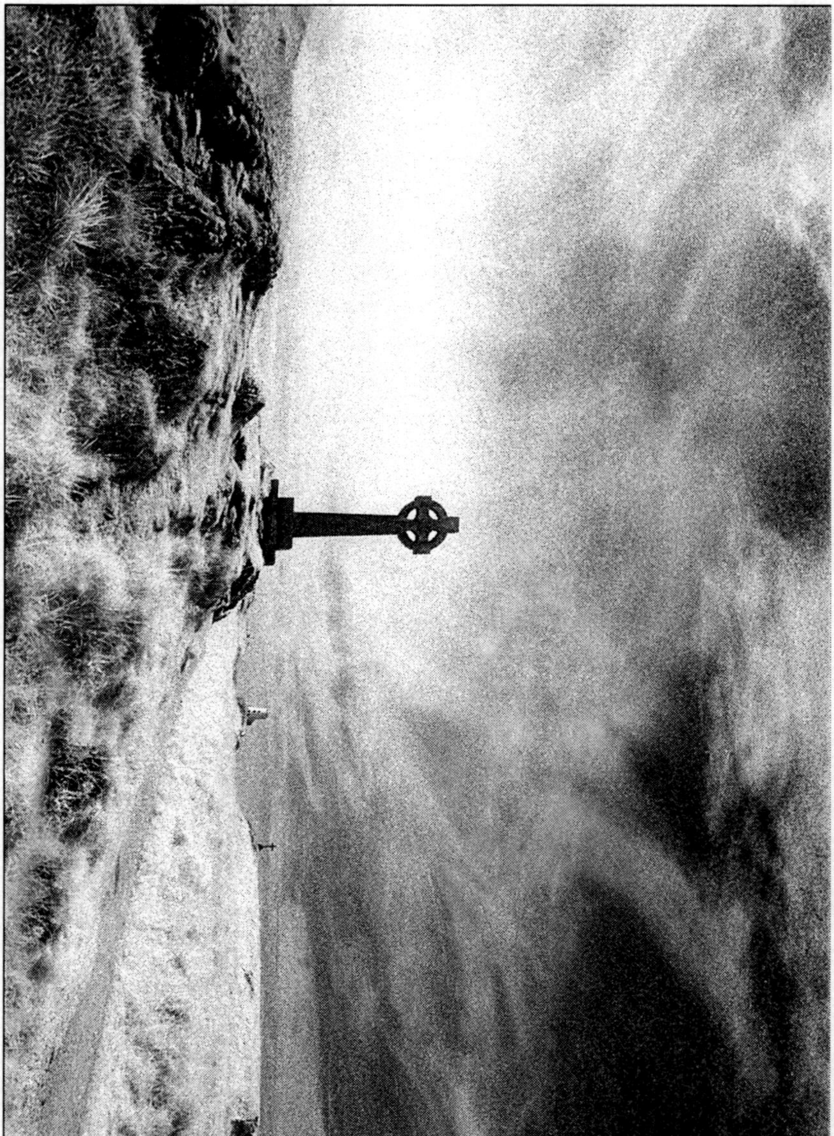

# 12. Weeds

Jesus told this parable:
"A farmer went out to sow his seed. As he was scattering the seed, some fell along the path and the birds came and ate it up. Some fell on rocky places, where it did not have much soil. It sprang up quickly, because the soil was shallow. But when the sun came up, the plants were scorched, and they withered because they had no root. Other seed fell among thorns, which grew up and choked the plants. Still other seed fell on good soil, where it produced a crop – a hundred, sixty or thirty times what was sown. He who has ears, let him hear.

"...The one who received the seed that fell among the thorns is the man who hears the word, but the worries of this life and the deceitfulness of wealth choke it, making it unfruitful."

(Matthew 13: v. 3–9 and v. 22)

Here's a picture in a few words. Up spring the young green shoots of faith, fresh and full of promise, then suddenly there are weeds around. Never noticed them coming but in no time at all they're around us and all that vitality is squeezed out.

Jesus calls the weeds 'the worries of this life', the things that everybody worries about – the rent, the mortgage, the house, the car, the job, the pension. There may be nothing wrong with them in themselves – in fact, quite the opposite – but they come with a snare: the power to choke the green shoots of faith and freedom.

He doesn't say we shouldn't have the responsibilities which most of us shoulder – not everyone can be a travelling preacher – but that they should be kept in their place. They are the stage on which our lives are lived. The drama is the life of faith – our relationship with God and, following from that, our relationship with others. This may seem pious to those who are struggling to make ends meet, or keep a marriage together, or bring up a family, or all these at once and more; but in the jungle of modern life a clear focus is essential to prevent the weeds from winning.

Jesus also calls the weeds 'the deceitfulness of wealth'. It's deceitful because it can't deliver what it promises: happiness, fulfilment, contentment. And it's a weed because it chokes – once it gets hold, you can't shake it off. You might think you can but you can't.

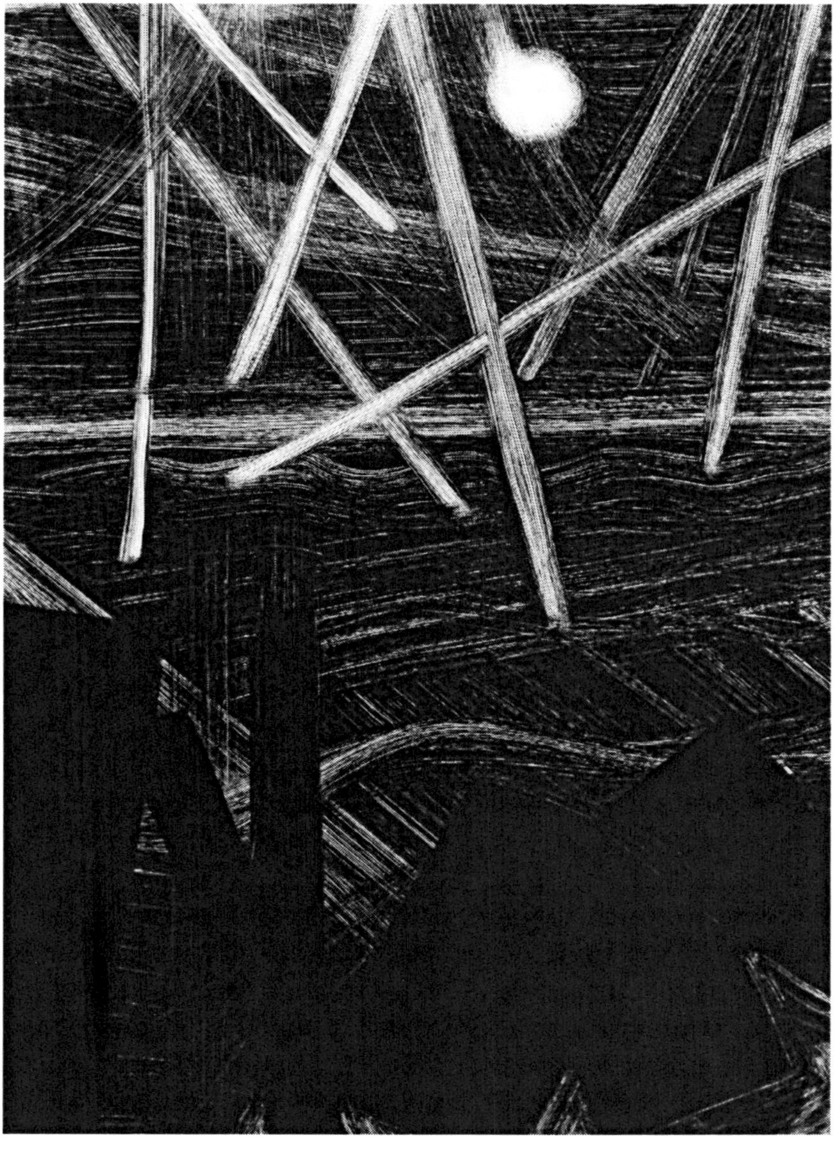

## 13. Spring into Life

"The hour has come for the Son of Man to be glorified. I tell you the truth, unless a grain of wheat falls to the ground and dies, it remains only a single seed. But if it dies, it produces many seeds. The man who loves his life will lose it, while the man who hates his life in this world will keep it for eternal life. Whoever serves me must follow me; and where I am, my servant also will be."
(John 12: v. 23–26)

Here Jesus strongly links the self-denial of the disciple with his own impending sacrifice. It is the only way to fruitfulness for both – self-denial for the disciple; the cross for Jesus. It is a scandalous travesty for Christians to reduce self-denial to giving up chocolates in Lent when for Jesus it meant crucifixion. If we want to serve him, as he says here, we have to follow him all the way.

These words contain the same self denial idea as the one in Chapter 10 and some of the same phrases as the quotation in Chapter 11, but the picture form is different. Here, the life of the disciple is compared to a seed which is buried in the ground and forgotten just as Jesus was crucified and buried. But then comes the glorious positive – for Jesus, resurrection; for the disciple, new and fruitful life.

No, again, it's not about giving up things for Lent; it's about the old self being put to death, buried and forgotten. And, no, it's not about going to church on Sundays; it's about living the new life of the kingdom which embraces everything we do.

So the choice is stark; we can either go it alone in search of our own dreams of fame and gold or we can take the plunge of self-denial into the dark but rich soil of discipleship and just see what comes up.

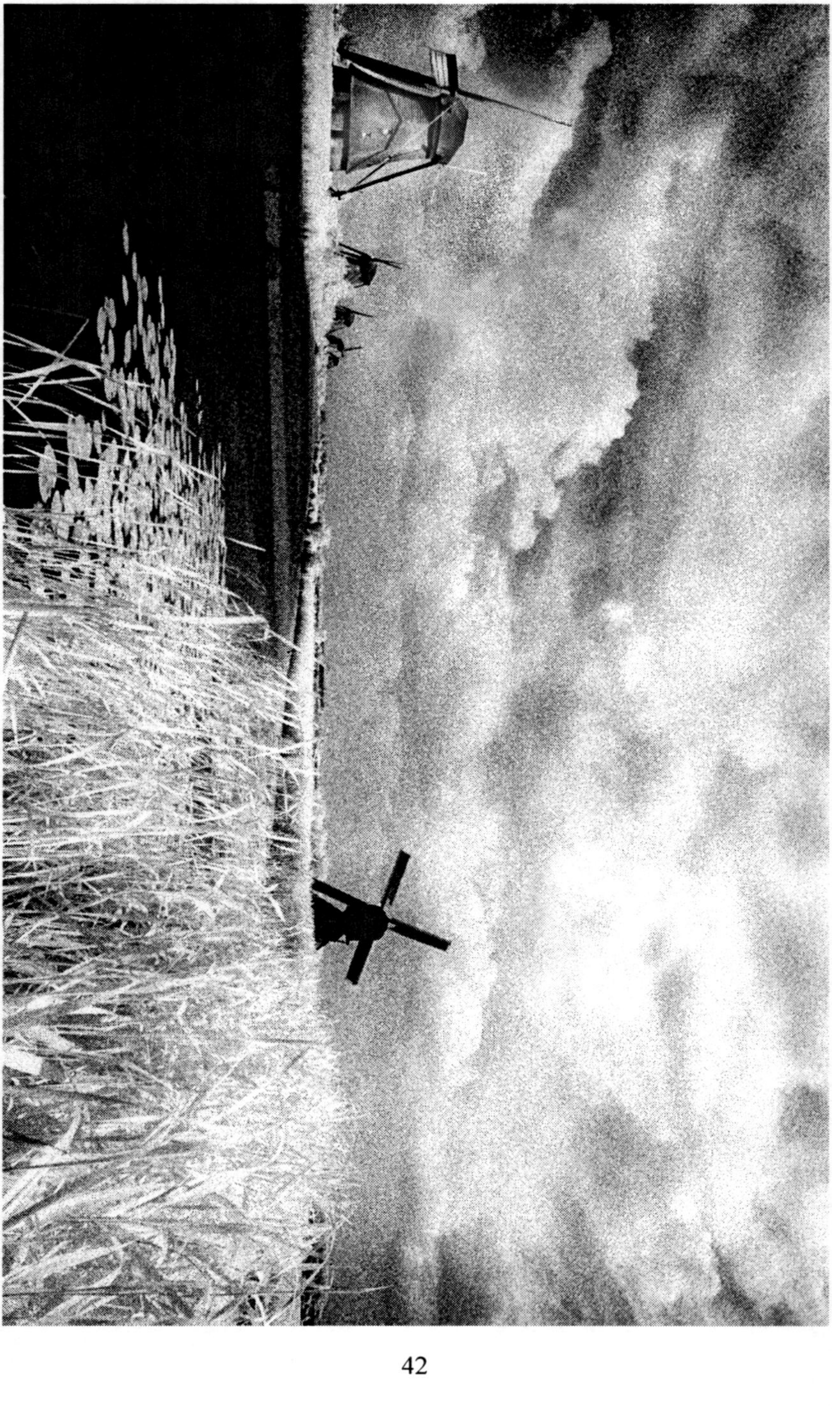

## 14. Too Much to Ask

A man came up to Jesus and asked, "Teacher, what good things must I do to get eternal life?"
… Jesus replied, "… If you want to enter life, obey the commandments."
"Which ones?" the man enquired.
Jesus replied, "'Do not murder, do not commit adultery, do not steal, do not give false testimony, honour your father and mother' and 'love your neighbour as yourself.'"
"All these I have kept," the young man said. "What still do I lack?"
Jesus answered, "If you want to be perfect, go, sell your possessions and give to the poor, and you will have treasure in heaven. Then come, follow me."
When the young man heard this, he went away sad, because he had great wealth.
(Matthew 19: v. 16–22)

This young chap has suffered from a bad press and vast over-exposure. If you have ventured into a church service more than once or twice then you are bound to have heard about him and he always gets the thumbs down because he was not prepared to pay the price of following Jesus. But the teeth of the story are always drawn because its obvious practical challenge is turned into a vague spiritual and emotional one. The congregation will be invited to 'give their whole lives to Christ' and not let anything stand in the way, without being told what that means in practical terms. They are never faced with the challenge which the young man faced – to sell up and give it all away. If they were, there might not be a congregation next week.

The fact is that Jesus was asking too much. The young chap really wanted to be a disciple but the down payment was too high and the returns too uncertain for anyone in their right mind to agree to it. "It might be all right for those fisherman and tax collector types because, well, they hadn't much to lose anyway. But me, in my position, err, no, not really – can't."

This is the problem for the rich or well-to-do. If you've got it, it's too good to let go, so you hang on to it. It's your security, your cosy nest egg, your treats for tomorrow. It's where your heart is. Jesus came for the poor because there was no point in him coming for the rich – their heart is elsewhere and not likely to move.

Stand up then, all you well-to-do Christians. How do you live with this one?

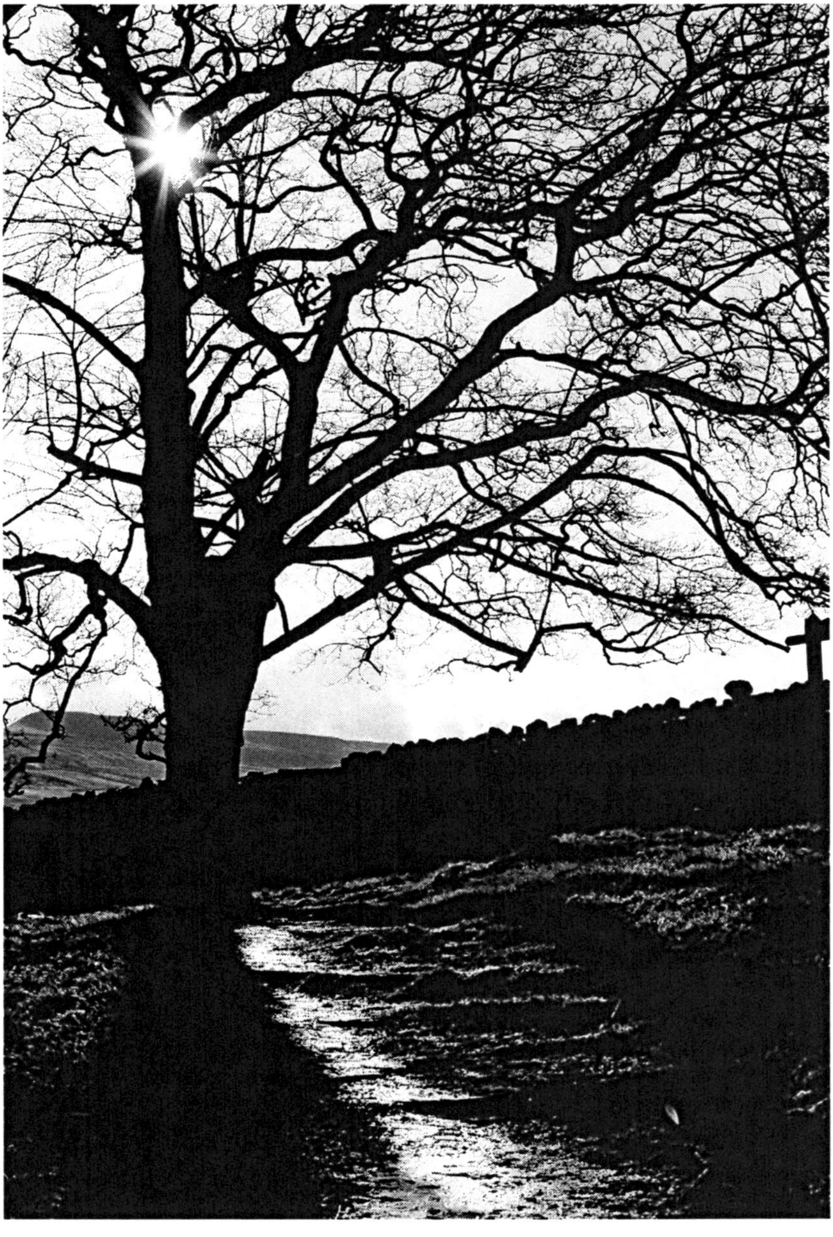

# 15. Zacchaeus

Jesus entered Jericho and was passing through. A man was there by the name of Zacchaeus; he was a chief tax collector and was wealthy. He wanted to see who Jesus was, but being a short man he could not, because of the crowd. So he ran ahead and climbed a sycamore-fig tree to see him, since Jesus was coming that way.

When Jesus reached the spot, he looked up and said to him, "Zacchaeus, come down immediately. I must stay at your house today." So he came down at once and welcomed him gladly.

All the people saw this and began to mutter, "He has gone to be the guest of a 'sinner'."

But Zacchaeus stood up and said to the Lord, "Look, Lord! Here and now I give half of my possessions to the poor, and if I have cheated anybody out of anything, I will pay back four times the amount."

Jesus said to him, "Today salvation has come to this house, because this man, too, is a son of Abraham. For the Son of Man came to seek and to save what was lost."

(Luke 19: v. 1–10)

This is an embarrassing story for many Christians. Zacchaeus wasn't told to repent and believe; he didn't have to promise to pray regularly or read the Bible every day or go to church twice on Sundays.

But with lots of people listening and hardly believing what

they heard, he promised to give his money away and more than repay those he had cheated. He ceased to be a getter and became a giver when he met Jesus in this glorious encounter. His statement wouldn't qualify him for membership of many of our churches but it was OK for Jesus: "Salvation has come to this house today." Marvellous.

Whatever made him do it? We don't know of course and we aren't told enough about him to make more than a guess. But he had certainly decided that his ill-gotten wealth had cost him more than it was worth and he didn't need Jesus to tell him that he couldn't be a disciple if it remained intact. He was a prisoner of his own making but here was his moment of release. He wasn't going to miss it for anything.

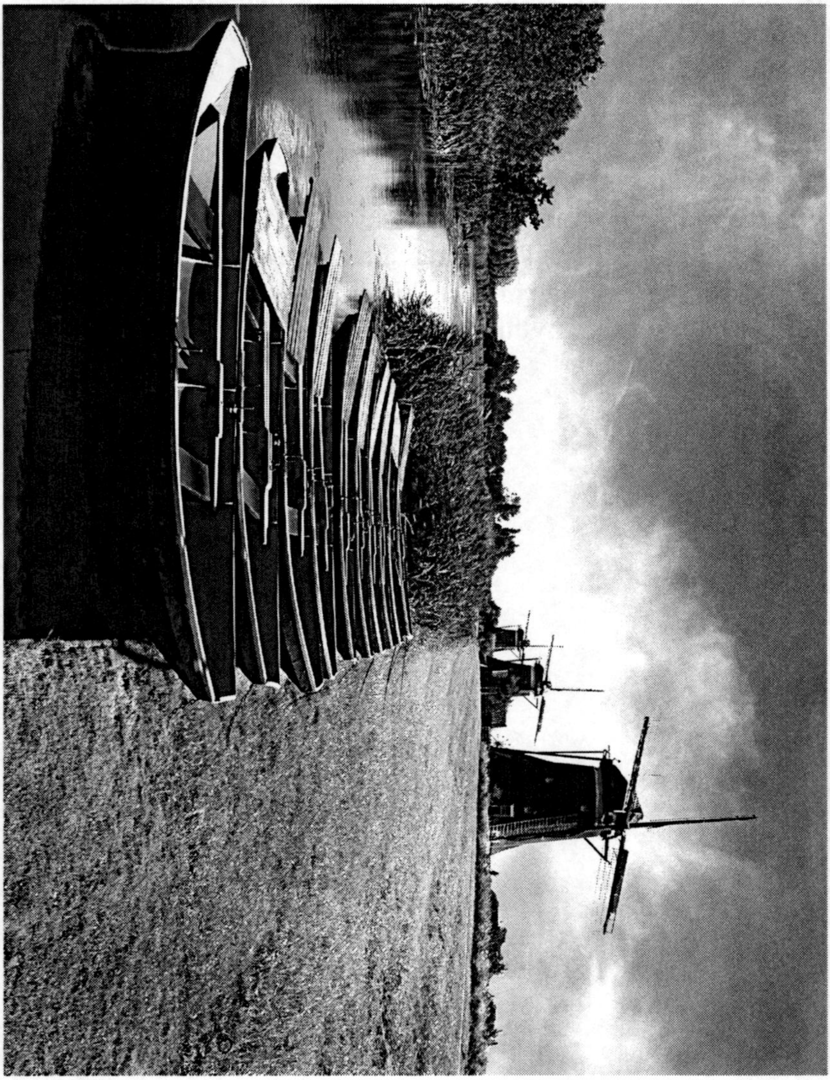

# 16. The Loophole

Then Jesus said to his disciples, "I tell you the truth, it is hard for a rich man to enter the kingdom of heaven. Again I tell you, it is easier for a camel to go through the eye of a needle than for a rich man to enter the kingdom of God."

When the disciples heard this, they were greatly astonished and asked, "Who then can be saved?"

Jesus looked at them and said, "With man this is impossible, but with God all things are possible."

(Matthew 19: v. 23–26)

(This is the conclusion to the event quoted in chapter 14 and perhaps it's a bit naughty to separate them. But it's such a well-known and misused quote that it deserves its own space.)

At last, here's a loophole; just what we need to wriggle out of these dreadful, all-embracing demands which Jesus makes. If a camel can get through, then so can we. It means that as long as God will work the impossible for us (and surely, he will) then we can keep all our wealth and possessions intact and still be his disciples.

That's more or less how we have drawn the sting from this poignant saying of Jesus, but it won't wash. According to Jesus it is humanly impossible for a rich person to enter the Kingdom of God – and Christians are very human. The Jesus kind of life is about giving and letting go, about love and generosity. The rich have devoted their lives to getting and keeping – that's why they are rich. They have chosen their way in preference to the kingdom way. They can't expect to enter the kingdom when they are heading in the opposite direction.

This doesn't mean that God can't save the rich. Zacchaeus was rich and Jesus welcomed him but look what he did with his savings.

The disciples were stunned by what Jesus had said and obviously thought it included them, even though they had made great sacrifices to follow him. Hence their question: "Who then can be saved?" Perhaps they recognised that there is no clear threshold between the rich and the rest of us. After all, wealth is relative and its base line is sufficiency. Once beyond that, we are soon into the temptations which plague the rich: greed, arrogance, acquisitiveness, independence from God and our friends. Only God can save us from the clutches of these. This is the 'impossible' which he is waiting to do for us.

Of course, we have our part to play as well – it's no use deliberately walking in the opposite direction to God's selfless way and expecting him to go with us. The only choice we have is whether to turn round or not.

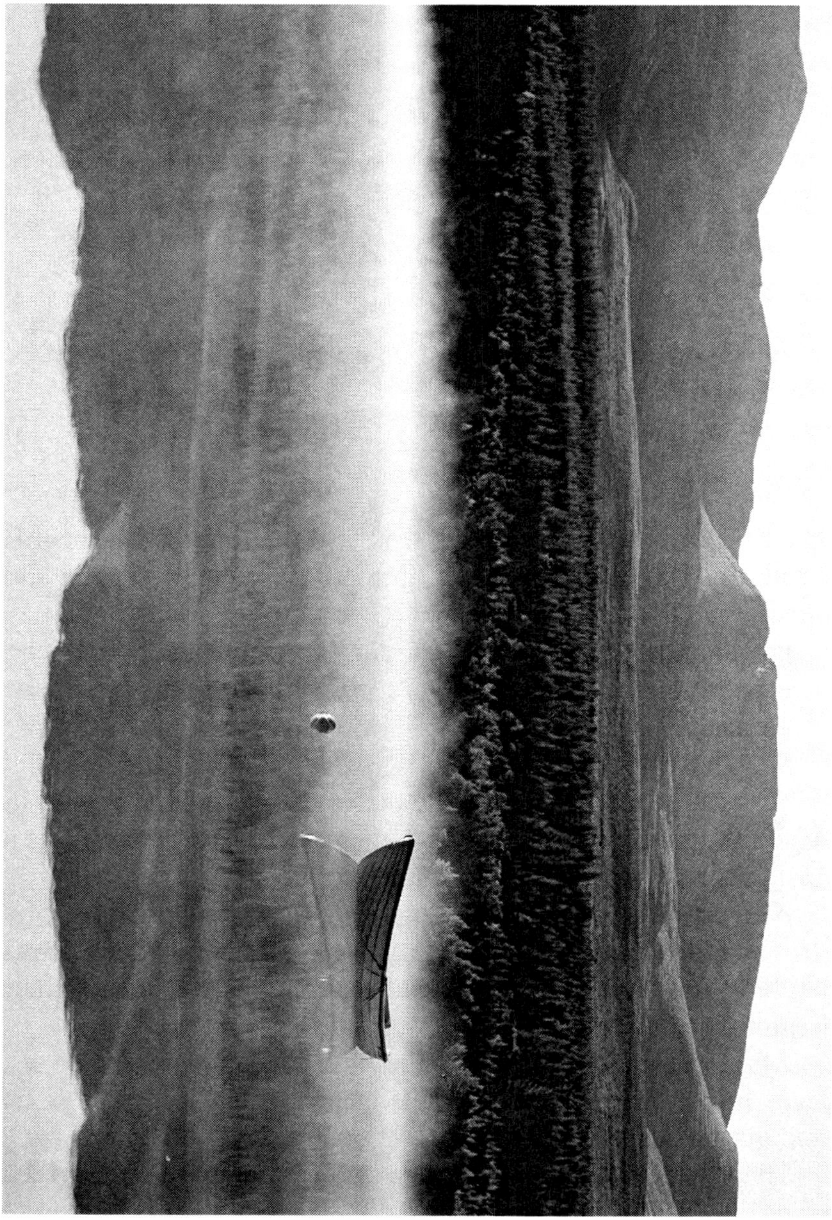

# 17. Asking the Impossible?

"Any of you who does not give up everything he has cannot be my disciple."

(Luke 14: v. 33)

This is a staggering statement. It is true that only Luke records it but, even so, it is difficult to ignore because it is so plain and direct.

Presumably, "everything" in our terms means house, car, investments, bank account, 'toys': in fact everything except the bare essentials.

So, what do we make of it?

We can, of course, reject the statement or at least ignore it. After all, it doesn't appear in the other gospels, so perhaps it is a mistake or a later insertion by some zealot.

Alternatively, we could dilute its impact for ourselves by stressing the dire times of famine and persecution in which it was written. You would hardly expect new converts to retain their wealth when all the others were starving.

Also, we could assume that the message is not meant for us. Jesus might have meant it for his close disciples, like those he sent out on the missionary journeys, rather than for you and me.

There were also other influences which may have affected the recording of what Jesus actually said. The early Christians were expecting Jesus to return and the world to come to an end at any time, so they would be getting rid of things ready for the big day rather than investing in something new.

Of course, we can obey the words to the letter and get rid of everything, but that is hardly a practical response. After all, there are some necessities of life and we have to provide for ourselves and our families if we possibly can. Nor is it a moral response. We can't abandon our responsibility to provide for ourselves and then expect others to do the providing for us. There is no suggestion anywhere in the gospels that Jesus requires the ordinary follower to opt out of the everyday economic activity of earning a living and caring for home and family.

On the other hand, he did make extreme demands of his twelve disciples and this could be one of them. Perhaps he was asking them if they had weighed up the true cost of following him, which could include their time, their wealth and even their lives.

The rest of us must try to weave this quotation into the whole of what Jesus had to say about wealth and possessions. For some, like the rich young man in Chapter 14 whose wealth stood between himself and the kingdom of God, it may mean just what it says – get rid of everything. For others it may mean we have to lighten our load in order to keep up with the leader. For those who can only dream of wealth it may mean: "beware, the dream is a mirage". To Jesus the lure of wealth was a barrier between us and the kingdom of God.

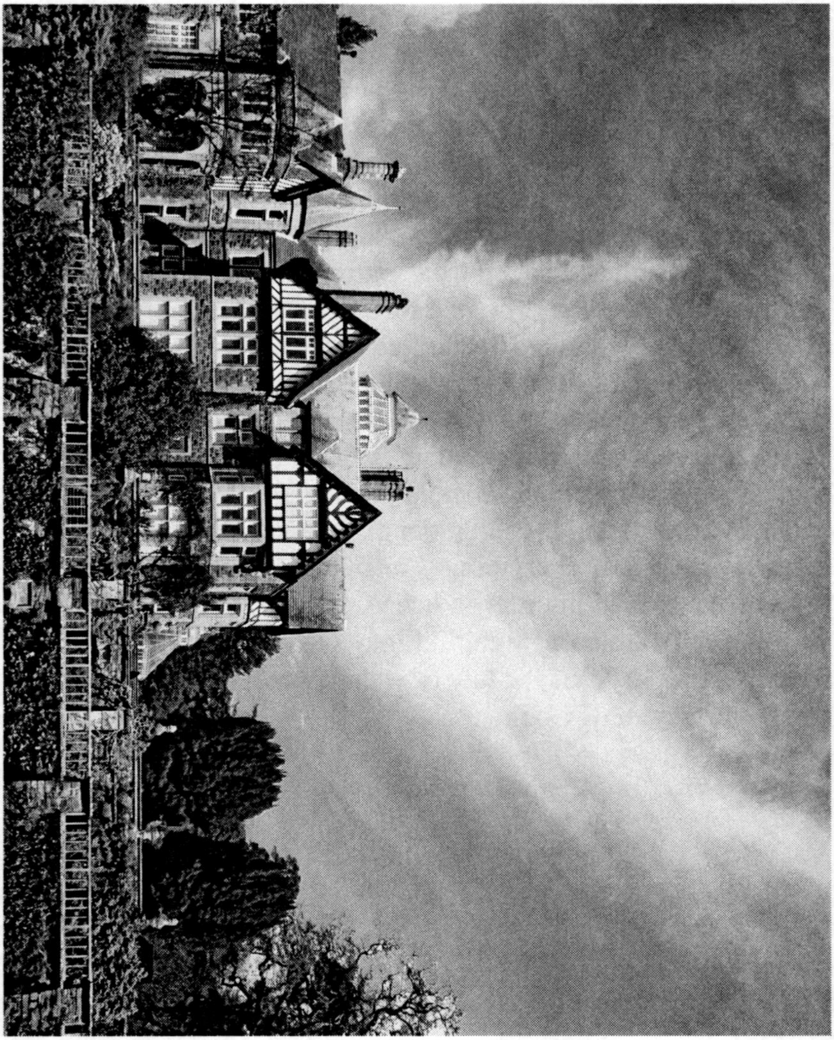

# 18. Top Priority

"The kingdom of heaven is like treasure hidden in a field. When a man found it, he hid it again, and then in his joy went and sold all that he had and bought that field."

"Again, the kingdom of heaven is like a merchant looking for fine pearls. When he found one of great value, he went away and sold everything he had and bought it."

(Matthew 13: v. 44–46)

These two short stories are about the kingdom of God and the value we place on getting there or belonging to it. To Jesus it meant everything. Whatever the price, it was worth it. Much better to be in the kingdom and destitute than out of it and well-off.

It is interesting to reflect on what Jesus meant by the kingdom of heaven (or the kingdom of God) – a study in itself. It certainly meant the rule of God in each person's life. Then there's the wider meaning for the disciple community of a shared faith and mission. Then an even wider one of the rule of God in society – local, national and international.

These are difficult stories for those of us who have other commitments and priorities. Do we have to lay such store on being a member of the kingdom of God, or of establishing it in society, that we will sacrifice everything else for it? Can't we just be normal, respectable Christians who live like everyone else but go to church on Sundays?

Obviously not. These stories are too demanding for any part-time Christianity. Finding, belonging to and establishing the kingdom of God were the top priorities that Jesus had in mind for his disciples. The only way to opt out is not to join in the first place.

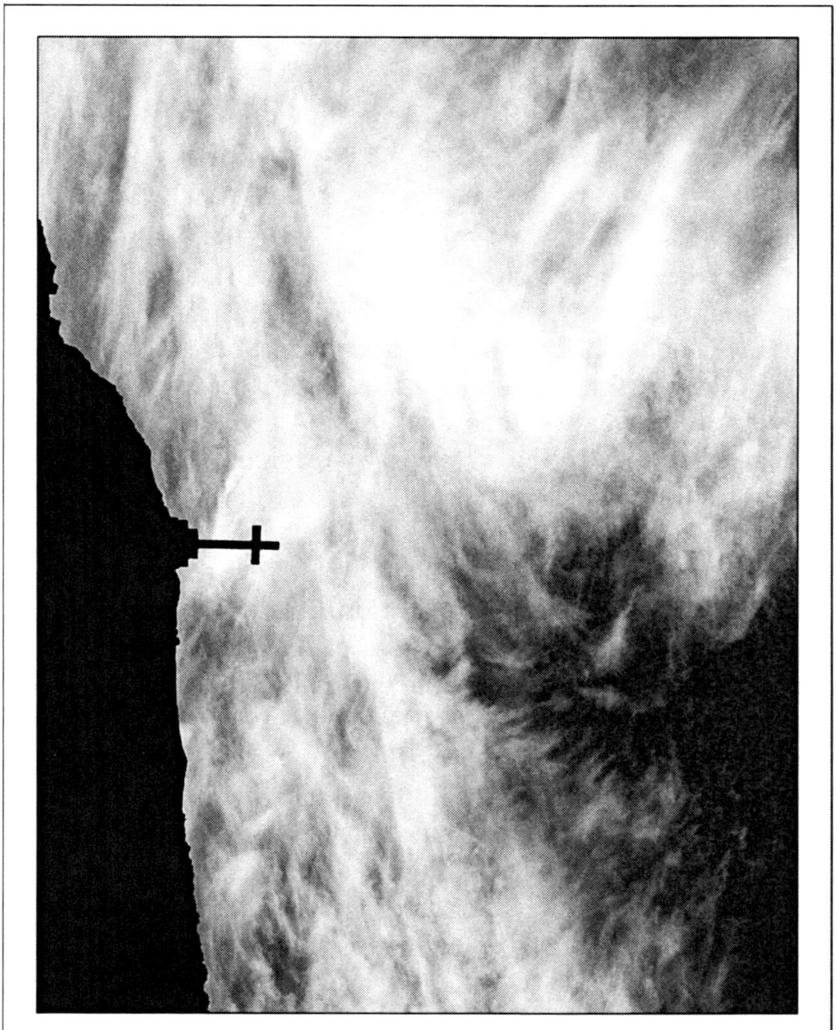

# 19. The Alternative

"Do not worry about your life, what you will eat or drink; or about your body, what you will wear. Is not life more important than food, and the body more important than clothes? Look at the birds of the air; they do not sow or reap or store away in barns, and yet your heavenly Father feeds them. Are you not much more valuable than they? Who of you by worrying can add a single hour to his life?

"And why do you worry about clothes? See how the lilies of the field grow. They do not labour or spin. Yet I tell you that not even Solomon in all his splendour was dressed like one of these. If that is how God clothes the grass of the field, which is here today and tomorrow is thrown into the fire, will he not much more clothe you, O you of little faith? So do not worry, saying, 'What shall we eat?' or 'What shall we drink?' or 'What shall we wear?' For the pagans run after all these things, and your heavenly Father knows that you need them. But seek first his kingdom and his righteousness, and all these things will be given to you as well. Therefore, do not worry about tomorrow, for tomorrow will worry about itself. Each day has enough trouble of its own."

(Matthew 6: v. 25–34)

This is one of the best-known passages from the Gospels and one of the most abused. We've drawn romantic pictures both on canvas and in our minds of Jesus picking flowers in an English country meadow and we've ignored the difficult and almost unacceptable message which he was trying to put across.

If we are honest, even those of us who call ourselves Christians take this message with a pinch of salt. For one thing, it's just not reasonable to compare our lives with the daisies in the field or the sparrows in the tree. It's true they do all right in their own little way and God does look after them; but we can't sunbathe or flit around all day and expect to get fed and clothed. We've been sowing and reaping, building and making things ever since Adam and Eve left the Garden of Eden. That's the way we earn a living and it's not going to change. And, of course, modern life brings its worries with it – mortgage, rent, car, holidays, education, health, redundancy etc. We can't be as free as the birds or as innocent and beautiful as the flowers.

We all know that it's no use worrying about these things because worry only drags us down into anxiety and then depression. But it's natural to worry. When life is full of uncertain outcomes we are bound to fear the worst even though we hope for the best. It's no use Jesus telling us not to worry unless he offers us an alternative.

Which he does. Everyone else is after wealth, success, status, acquisitions, or simply food and clothing – as in this quotation – but the Christian is after the kingdom of God. The rub is that we are not happy with this. Deep down, we don't believe that the kingdom of God is our natural destiny – the only experience in which we can be truly happy and find our real selves. We are not content to lose out compared to others. After all, they are after something tangible and might well achieve it. Christians are after something intangible and it might end up as a wild goose chase or, at least, seem so to others.

Jesus justifies his challenge to our way of thinking by claiming that God will provide for our needs just like he does for the flowers and birds. The difficulty is that this doesn't seem to square with the facts. How many early Christians sold everything and threw in their lot with the Church only to meet an untimely end in the persecutions and famines? And how many thousands of people across the world today lift up their hands in a desperate prayer for food only to bury their little ones who have died for lack of it? It would be evil to suggest that they perished because their parents were not really seeking the kingdom of God.

Jesus was well aware of the precarious economic situation of many of his followers and he knew the risks they were taking by their allegiance to him. He knew they would be hard up, rejected and even killed and he also foresaw the impending national disasters. So how could he say that God would always provide?

Well, there is a sense in which God always provides as he promised to Noah long ago: "there will always be a seed time and a harvest" and we have to trust him for that. He knows there are problems of fair distribution and proper use of the world's resources, not to mention war, and Christians can't expect to be immune from any of these. But still he wants us to trust him to provide while we concentrate on seeking his kingdom because this is the way to liberated living, free from the lure of things which all the world runs after. How free are you?

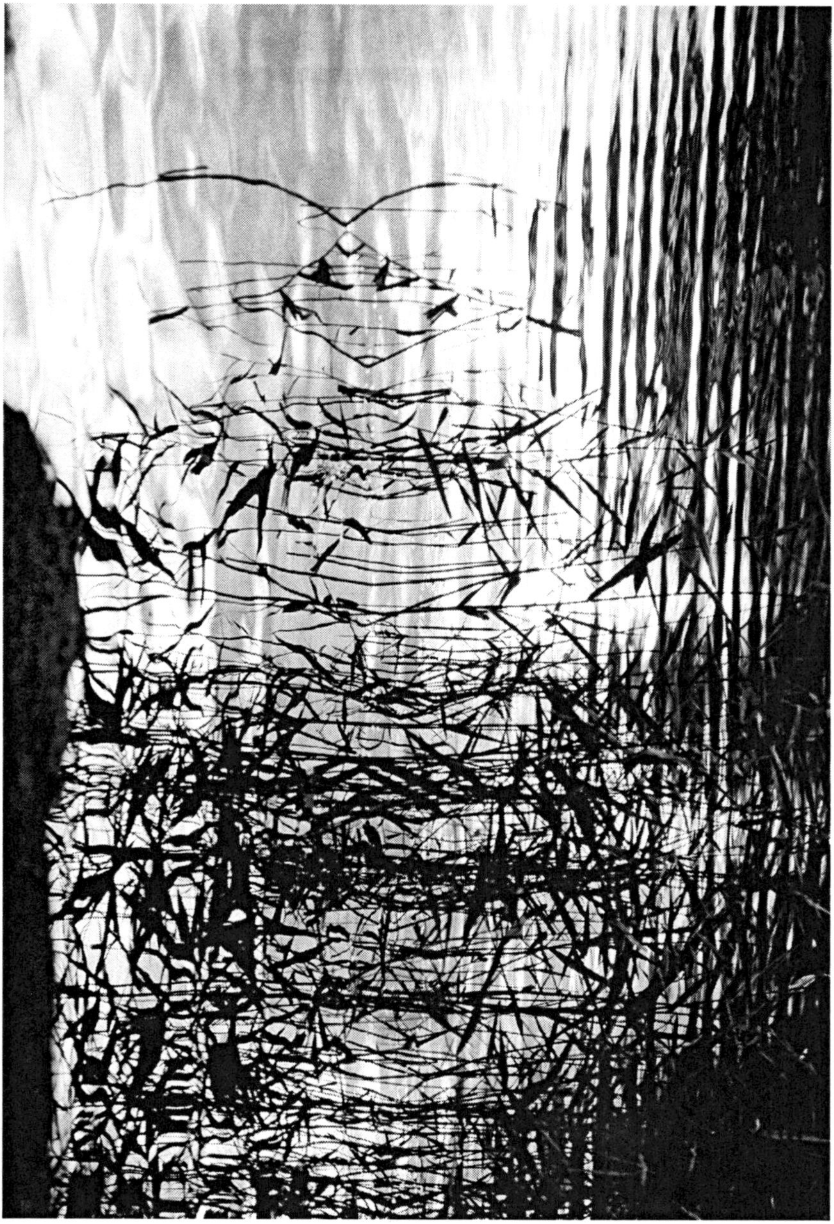

## 20. The Main Job

As Jesus walked beside the Sea of Galilee, he saw Simon and his brother Andrew casting a net into the lake, for they were fishermen. "Come, follow me," Jesus said, "and I will make you fishers of men." At once they left their nets and followed him.
When he had gone a little farther, he saw James son of Zebedee and his brother John in a boat, preparing their nets. Without delay he called them, and they left their father Zebedee in the boat with the hired men and followed him.
(Mark 1: v. 16–20)

This must be a brief summary of what actually happened. Both Luke and John add a few more details in their gospels but Mark's brevity seems to add to the drama.
According to John's Gospel, Andrew and Peter had already met Jesus. James and John would, no doubt, have heard about him but even so, this was all a bit sudden. Here is Jesus, strolling along by the lake; he spots both sets of brothers in the boats and says "follow me". And they do. Not a word about poor old Zebedee left high and dry with the family business. He thought he had some really good boys who were working hard to build it up. Then, whoosh! They're off with not so much as a wave.
It all may seem highly irresponsible to us. We know that Peter was married and perhaps the others were. Whatever did their wives say? Who would pay the bills and do the jobs around the house?

What about the mortgage or the rent? Zebedee would probably have to take on more hired labour in place of the brothers – all extra expense. The brothers couldn't expect to get paid if they didn't put in the work. And what about the future of the business if they had gone for good?

Well, we know that it wasn't as clean a break as it may seem from this story because Jesus and the disciples had easy access to fishing boats throughout the Gospel stories and they were probably the boats belonging to these two families. Perhaps the disciples were with Jesus for only part of the time and did their fishing jobs at other times. It is also true that times were different to ours and it may be that a travelling preacher and healer would get plenty of financial support – we know that Judas, the betrayer, looked after the money, so they must have had some kind of income. But, even so, what they did had massive financial implications for themselves and their families and this fact doesn't get a mention in the Bible text. For Jesus, these disciple brothers, and the gospel writers the economic realities of life were secondary to the main task in hand.

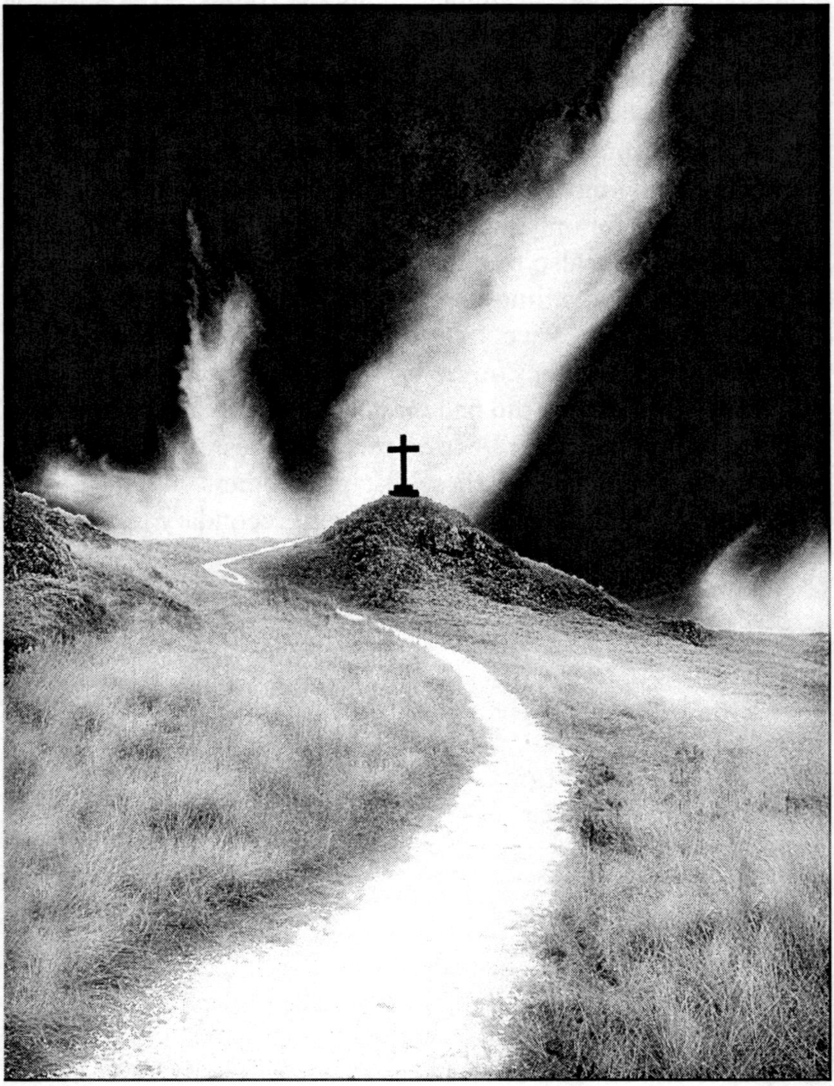

# 21. Travelling Light

When Jesus had called the Twelve together, he gave them power and authority to drive out all demons and to cure diseases, and he sent them out to preach the kingdom of God and to heal the sick. He told them: "Take nothing for the journey – no staff, no bag, no bread, no money, no extra tunic."

(Luke 9: v. 1–3)

This is only one of four possible quotes about the same or similar events and they all differ in detail though not in essence. For instance in Mark's record they were told to take a staff whereas here in Luke's, they were told not to. If we stick to the common ground, they certainly travelled light – very light – on their preaching and healing tours.

Jesus didn't instruct them to travel light just to make life tough for them, as in a tribal initiation test or cold dormitories in a public school. Rather, he knew they couldn't preach the good news to the poor while living in the lap of luxury; that if they had no earthly support system they would have to depend on God; and the less they were encumbered, the more they could concentrate on the job in hand.

But has it any relevance for us? It probably has if we have chosen to be ministers of religion. Jesus clearly expected those he had chosen to spread the message to leave everything behind, at least for the time being. It is also clear that some were chosen for the job and others were not.

This fits in quite well with our situation where only a few enter the full-time Christian ministry or priesthood while the rest of us support them. This doesn't mean we can leave evangelism to the professionals – there is no such thing as an amateur Christian. Nor can we expect them to bear hardship while we live it up and toss them the odd donation. It doesn't mean either that we have to be destitute in order to follow him, or who would support the few?

So has it any relevance for the rest of us Christians who have an ordinary place in society with a job, a family and a home? It probably does because we, too, preach a gospel to the poor. We need to be conscious of our dependency on God and we need to keep our focus on the kingdom of God. We can't do these things if our hearts are set on getting and keeping and it's this different focus which sets the disciple apart.

## 22. Nest Egg

""Do not store up for yourselves treasures on earth, where moth and rust destroy and thieves break in and steal. But store up for yourselves treasures in heaven, where moth and rust do not destroy, and where thieves do not break in and steal. For where your treasure is, there your heart will be also." (Matthew 6: v. 19–21)

Elderly folks often excuse their extravagance on this or that luxury by saying, "well, you can't take it with you". And you may have met fundraisers using the same saying and adding, "but you can send it on in advance" - by contributing to their particular good cause. It is not quite the same as what Jesus was saying because the fundraisers are targetting the treasures of those who already have one whereas Jesus tells us that it's better not to make one in the first place.

We know we can't take it with us – we leave as empty as when we came - but it's still nice to have it while we are here, tucked away for that rainy day or perhaps for that treat we have been promising ourselves for so long. In any case, we can always leave it to the kids, so it's not wasted even if we go before our time.

But the message from Jesus is: don't make a pile in the first place. Your wealth will separate you from God and your friends. Aquisitiveness is an incurable and terminal illness - once it gets hold you can't shake it off. There's a crushingly sad moment in Dickens' story 'A Christmas Carol' when Scrooge's sweetheart ends their engagement with, "Another idol has displaced me – a golden one". He had exchanged love for wealth, a fatal choice.

Now, we know that we live in a different age and culture from Palestine 2000 years ago and that we have some responsibility to provide for ourselves when we we are too old to work but we must avoid the dangers of life and love being squeeezed out of us by the mirage of wealth.

Also woven into this little saying is the idea of reward. This is very much out of fashion and you won't hear much about it in our churches but it is written large in what Jesus had to say. We have built the Christian message around the free grace of God, which means that you can't earn salvation – only God can give it to you. Unfortunately, we have ditched the idea of reward in the process because the two seem contradictory.

But they need cementing together. The response of the believer to God's gift of salvation is delight, worship and a new, refreshing focus on Jesus and his kingdom. It's the selfless deeds naturally flowing from that focus which earn the rewards. Read all about it.

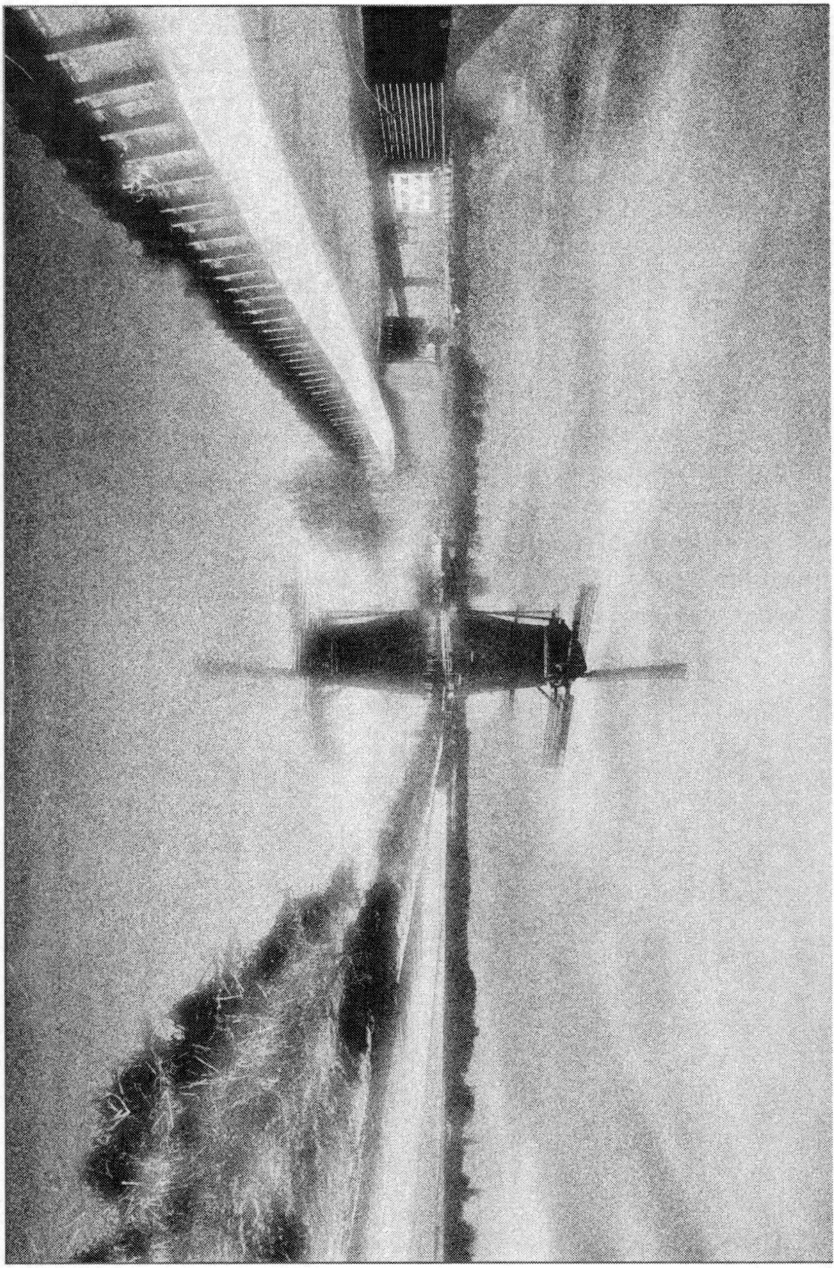

## 23. Loan Repayment

"Love your enemies, do good to them, and lend to them without expecting to get anything back. Then your reward will be great, and you will be the sons of the Most High, because he is kind to the ungrateful and wicked."

(Luke 6: v. 35)

Here's an easy way into the kingdom of God: never mind trying to squeeze through the eye of a needle; you only have to lend to your enemies and you are in.

That's not all he is saying here, of course, but he typically moves from the principle to the practical. We might try to hide behind the vagueness of 'love' and 'goodness' but lending is down to earth and hits us in our pockets – especially when we don't get repaid and especially when it is to our enemies. When did you last do a kindness to your enemy? It's not easy, is it? But "God is kind to the ungrateful and wicked" and he expects us to be the same.

Here, again, is the principle and promise of reward and, as we noted in the last chapter, it is found all over the Gospels. It's even in the Lord's Prayer – we can expect God's forgiveness but we must be forgiving too. It is the whole essence of the Judgement story in Matthew's Gospel where the King separates the good from the bad on the simple basis that the good people loved and cared for their neighbours in selfless practical ways and the bad people did not (see Chapter 25). He even teases the Pharisees with it when they are fussing about being ritually clean: "Give… to the poor, and everything will be ritually clean for you." (Luke 11: v. 41 (GNB))

The rewards are nearly always spiritual. In this quote the ultimate reward of a place in the kingdom of God is on offer. Elsewhere, as in the judgement story, the rewards are only dispensed in Heaven. There is never any hint from Jesus that following him will bring wealth or what we call success. In fact the very opposite is promised time and time again. If the leader was treated so badly, why should the followers expect a better deal?

Before Jesus came, the Jews believed that God would reward goodness and devotion with all the good things of life. It followed, of course, that prosperity was a sign of God's blessing and approval. There are lots of Christians about today who think just the same: they are buried in the Old Testament and blind to the teachings of Jesus, not to mention his lifestyle and his sacrifice.

But is a spiritual reward enough of a carrot to tempt us to be his followers or to motivate us to do and be what he expects? Probably not. In our materialistic age, 'reward' means hard cash or at least payment in kind and certainly not something as wishy-washy as a spiritual reward or 'pie in the sky when you die'. Unfortunately for us, such a response merely shows how far removed we are from what he has in mind for us. For him, life is a spiritual journey – the material things are its necessary props. Jesus wants us to live his kind of life simply because it is the best for us. Which will you choose? His way is costly and risky but exciting as well. Don't dither – decide.

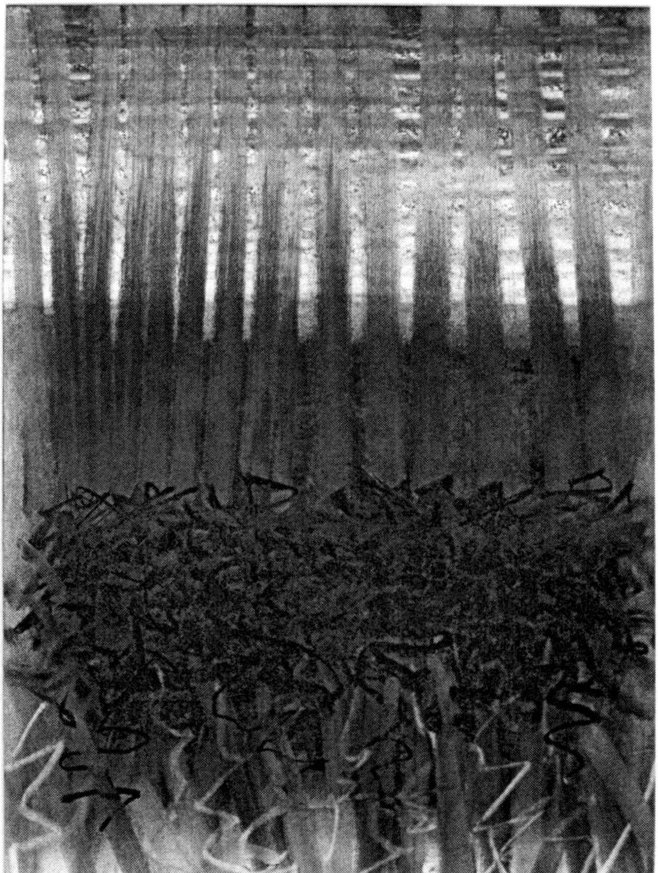

# 24. Ours to Share

"Woe to you who are rich, for you have already received your comfort."

(Luke 6: v. 24)

This is a difficult saying. It all depends on whether the rich includes me. There's always someone better off than me so perhaps it means someone else and I can escape the woe. But Jesus probably meant anyone with an excess of income over their needs, which would include an awful lot of us.

You could draw the sting from the quote just a little by observing that only Luke records the 'woes'. As we noticed in Chapter 4, Luke seems to have it in for the rich much more than Matthew does. Both record the blessings but only Luke adds these nasty little woes.

But it is not so easy to dismiss because we have already met the same principle in the story of the successful farmer (Chapter 9) and we shall meet it again in Chapter 28: the story of the rich man and Lazarus. It is also present in the sad meeting of Jesus and the rich young man who turned away (Chapter 14) as well as in the happy one with Zacchaeus who did just the opposite (Chapter 15).

At least this statement is plain and simple – the rich are in trouble because they have decided to enjoy the comforts of their wealth here and now. And why should they not enjoy it? After all, they have probably earned it; it's theirs, so why shouldn't they enjoy it?

Well, there are a few reasons for those who dare to look but they cut across our lifestyle and pattern of discipleship.

Firstly, the rich have chosen the wrong reward. The life which Jesus wants us to aim for and enjoy is about giving, not getting and keeping. You can't have both and the rich have chosen the latter.

Then there is the principle, not new but still revolutionary, that the excess which we are able to earn or gather doesn't belong to us except to give away. This is the practical summary of Jesus' teaching on wealth and possessions and it was the financial foundation of the early Church.

This comes as a bit of a shock to our Western, individualistic way of thinking but there is great logic in it. If you list all the factors which have contributed to a person's success – health, education, intelligence, breeding, early experience, character, luck – you can see the rich didn't earn them: they are gifts – gifts from God. God didn't give gifts to the gifted for their own enjoyment alone, otherwise you would have to say that he withheld gifts from the less able in order to condemn them to disadvantage, which can't be right.

Finally, we shall be rich in heaven. Till then, how can we, whom God has gifted, wallow in the fruits of our talents while our neighbour is in dreadful need?

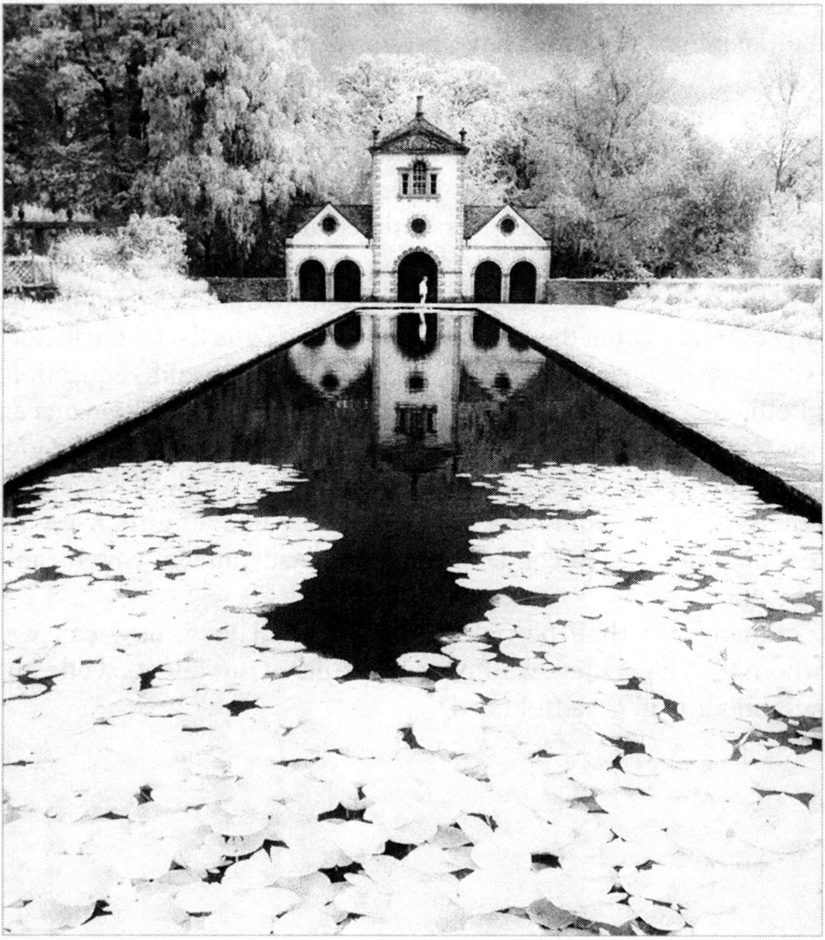

## 25. God's Entrepreneur

"[The kingdom of heaven] will be like a man going on a journey, who called his servants and entrusted his property to them. To one he gave five talents of money, to another two talents, and to another one talent, each according to his ability. Then he went on his journey. The man who had received the five talents went at once and put his money to work and gained five more. So also, the one with the two talents gained two more. But the man who had received the one talent went off, dug a hole in the ground and hid his master's money.

"After a long time the master of those servants returned and settled accounts with them. The man who had received the five talents brought the other five. 'Master,' he said, 'you entrusted me with five talents. See, I have gained five more.'

"His master replied, 'Well done, good and faithful servant! You have been faithful with a few things; I will put you in charge of many things. Come and share your master's happiness!'

"The man with the two talents also came. 'Master,' he said, 'you entrusted me with two talents; see, I have gained two more.'

"His master replied, 'Well done, good and faithful servant! You have been faithful with a few things; I will put you in charge of many things. Come and share your master's happiness!'

"Then the man who had received the one talent came. 'Master,' he said, 'I knew that you are a hard man, harvesting where you have not sown and gathering where you have not scattered seed. So I was afraid and went out and hid your talent in the ground. See, here is what belongs to you.'

"His master replied, 'you wicked, lazy servant! So you knew that I harvest where I have not sown and gather where I have not scattered seed? Well then, you should have put my money on deposit with the bankers, so that when I returned I would have received it back with interest.

"'Take the talent from him and give it to the one who has the ten talents. For everyone who has will be given more, and he will have an abundance. Whoever does not have, even what he has will be taken from him. And throw that worthless servant outside, into the darkness, where there will be weeping and gnashing of teeth.'"

(Matthew 25: v. 14–30)

This is a simple, well known story but it is far from a favourite because it seems, at first sight, to be out of step with the rest of Jesus' teaching. Elsewhere, he counsels us to be meek, to choose the last place, to give and not to grab for ourselves, but here it's the pusher, the entrepreneur, who gets the medals.

Or so it seems – but it is the wrong interpretation because it overlooks the fact that these servants were slaves. The two successful ones didn't slave away in order to feather their own nests. The money they earned was for their master, not for themselves. They did benefit from their efforts, of course, but their rewards were entirely at the master's discretion.

Have you ever met an entrepreneur who was working for someone else? The whole ethic of our economic system is based on personal gain at the expense of the competitor and it is contrary to Christian teaching. But you don't have to be an entrepreneur to have a single-minded passion for the task in hand and that reckless willingness to risk everything which is sometimes the only chance of success. These were trademarks of Jesus in his day as well as of today's business entrepreneur and have been trademarks of his true followers ever since. The servants in this story worked hard to please their master and for no other reason.

So the message of this story is not about building up a nest egg for our retirement and getting a pat on the back from God for doing it, but about using the gifts he has given us in his service. When we meet him, he won't want to hear that at the peak of our careers we owned a detached house, two up-market cars and a cottage in the country. He will want to know what we have done with the gifts he has given us and how we used them to establish the kingdom of God on earth.

And it is no use complaining that he didn't give us much to work on.

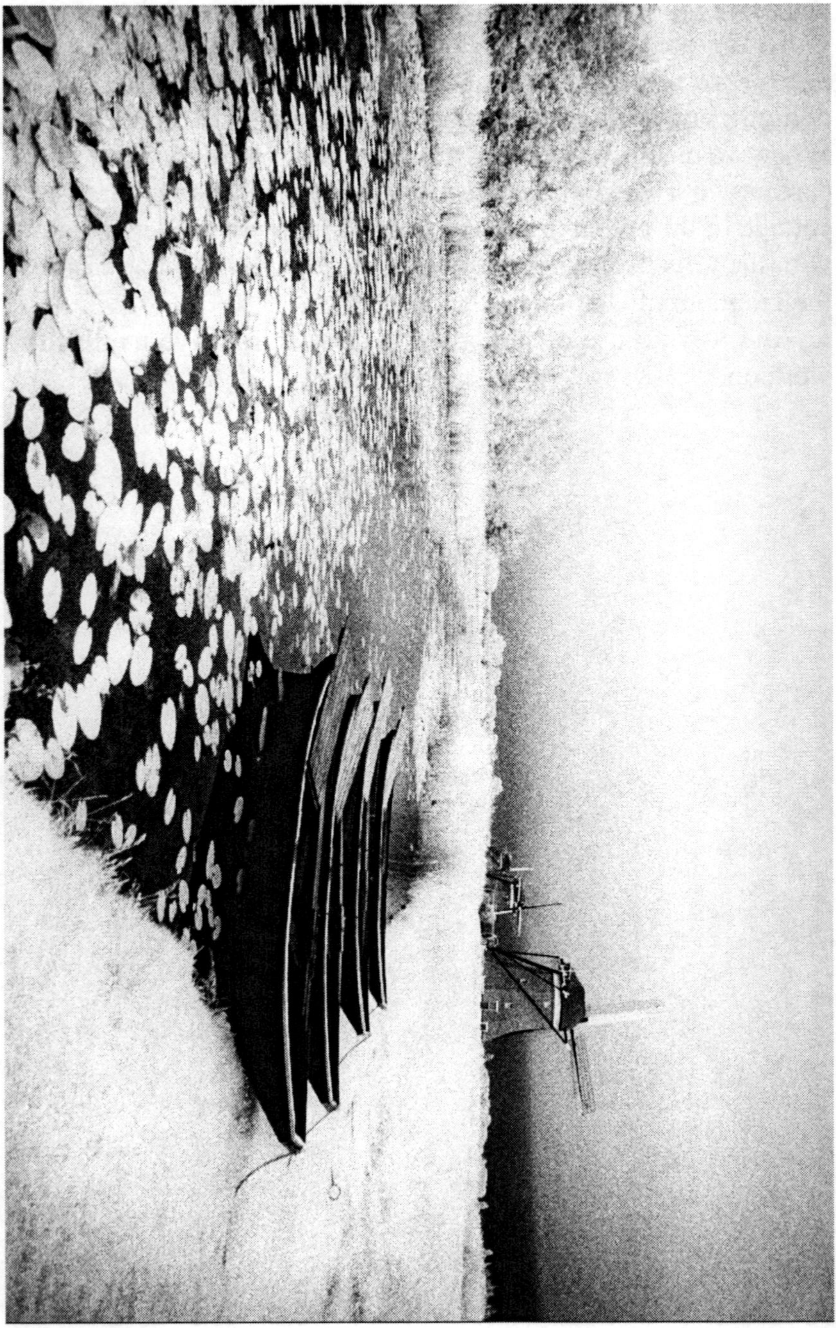

# 26. Do-gooders

"When the Son of Man comes in all his glory, and all the angels with him, he will sit on his throne in heavenly glory. All the nations will be gathered before him, and he will separate the people one from another as a shepherd separates the sheep from the goats. He will put the sheep on his right and the goats on his left.

"Then the King will say to those on his right, 'Come, you who are blessed by my Father; take your inheritance, the kingdom prepared for you from the creation of the world. For I was hungry and you gave me something to eat, I was thirsty and you gave me something to drink, I was a stranger and you invited me in, I needed clothes and you clothed me, I was sick and you looked after me, I was in prison and you came to visit me.'

"Then the righteous will answer him, 'Lord, when did we see you hungry and feed you, or thirsty and give you something to drink? When did we see you a stranger and invited you in, or needing clothes and clothe you? When did we see you sick or in prison and go to visit you?'

"The King will reply, 'I tell you the truth, whatever you did for one of the least of these brothers of mine, you did for me.'"

(Matthew 25: v. 31–40)

The second half of the story (v. 41–46) in which those on the left get sent to eternal fire for not doing these good things, is a mirror image of the first.

This is the last of three stories in Matthew 25 about the end of the present age when Jesus will come as Judge. The first, the story of the wise and foolish bridesmaids (v. 1–13) is about being ready when he comes. The second, the Parable of the Talents, the subject of Chapter 25 above, is about what we have done with God's investment. Then comes this one about the kind of return God is looking for. [1]

The most startling thing about the story is the absence of any religious qualifications which might be required in order to secure a place in heaven. There is no mention of going to church, of saying your prayers or reading the Bible. You don't have to be a theologian or an evangelist; you don't have to have ecstatic experiences or display your spiritual gifts of healing or teaching.

But you do have to be good. Not the hollow sort of goodness that merely smiles sweetly and says the right kind of things, but an active goodness which reaches out to other people in good deeds. The sort of goodness that Jesus demands doesn't care who the recipient is, doesn't count how often or how much, doesn't make a song and dance about it but comes from the heart and can't even be remembered. Heaven will be full of such people.

Unfortunately for those of us who like to inhabit the grey areas of life, this story doesn't offer one. This is consistent with the whole of the Bible and particularly with all that Jesus had to say. We are on one side or the other, in or out, for or against – there is no room on the fence. This might seem unreasonable because even the worst of us do the odd good deed and the best of us have plenty of warts. But what we do and how we do it is determined by what we are like inside. As Jesus says elsewhere, "The good man brings good things out of the good stored up in him."

---

[1] There are other passages and sayings about judgement in the Bible which give a different emphasis to this one and it is only fair to mention them. In John's Gospel, it is belief in Jesus as the Son and Saviour which is all important: "Whoever believes in [the Son] shall have eternal life"

(Chapter 3 v. 16). Later on in the Letters and in Revelation the emphasis is on purity – the faithful have been made pure by Christ's redemptive act. However, these can be seen to complement rather than contradict what Jesus had to say about judgement in the first three Gospels and particularly in this great story.

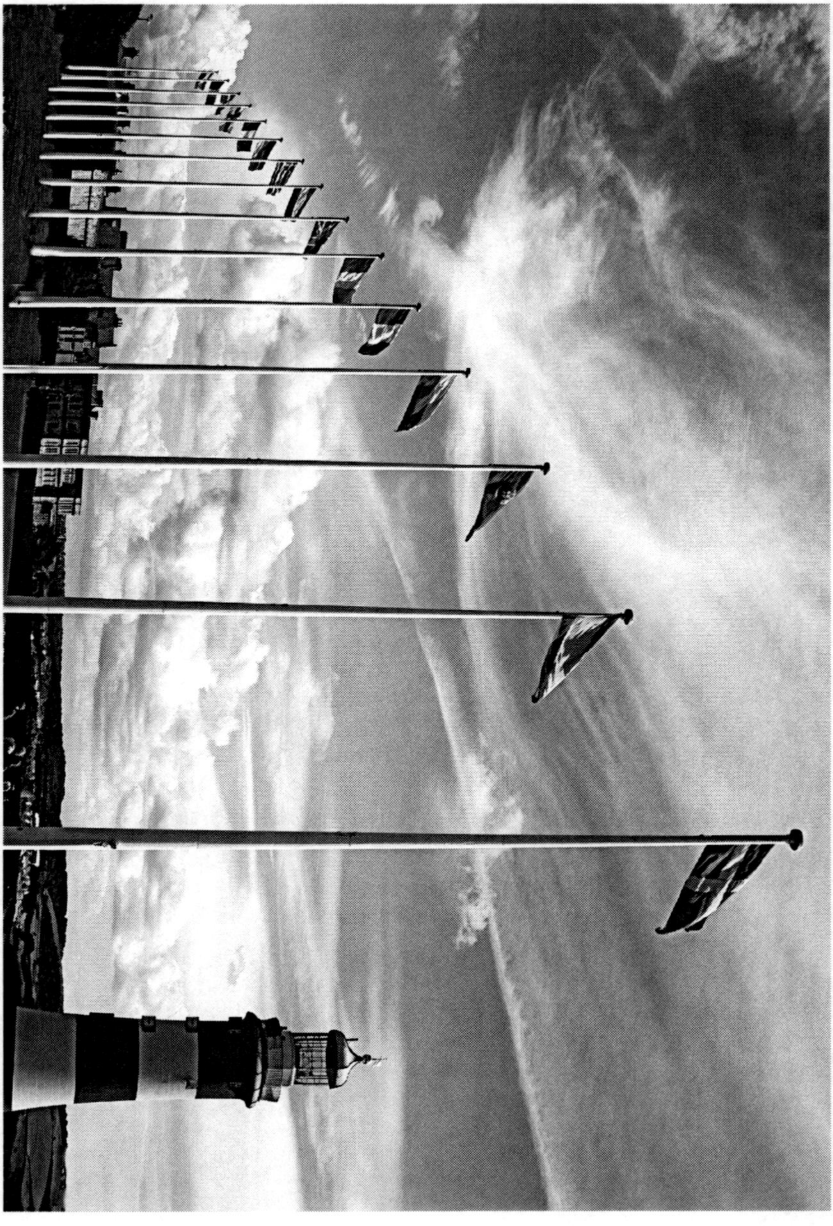

# 27. The Great Reversal

"So the last will be first, and the first will be last."
(Matthew 20 v. 16)

This is a recurring theme in what Jesus had to say. It started before he was born in Mary's song: "He has brought down rulers from their thrones but has lifted up the humble." In the new age there will be a great reversal of fortunes – the meek will inherit the earth and the poor will be rich. But the principle applies to the here and now as well because he teaches his disciples to be childlike and to take the attitude of a servant in their relationships with each other – most powerfully when he washes their feet just before his death.

This principle of meekness is not a favourite with many Christians. It's all right in the pulpit perhaps but it's no good in the real world on Monday where it's the go-getter, the pusher, the outside-lane man or woman who gets the medals and turns the heads.

But such an ethic has no place in the kingdom of the Servant. To Jesus, the meek will inherit the earth because they will do a better job and wealth, fame and power are false gods which have a very hollow ring when we eventually get hold of them.

We have all fallen for the lie that meekness is inconsistent with determination, conviction and passion – when it isn't at all. Meekness is a willingness to serve, not a readiness to back down. It is a willingness to recognise the dignity of the other person, not a lack of conviction. It's just a harder line to hold. But Jesus never said it was easy to be his kind of person – look what happened to him.

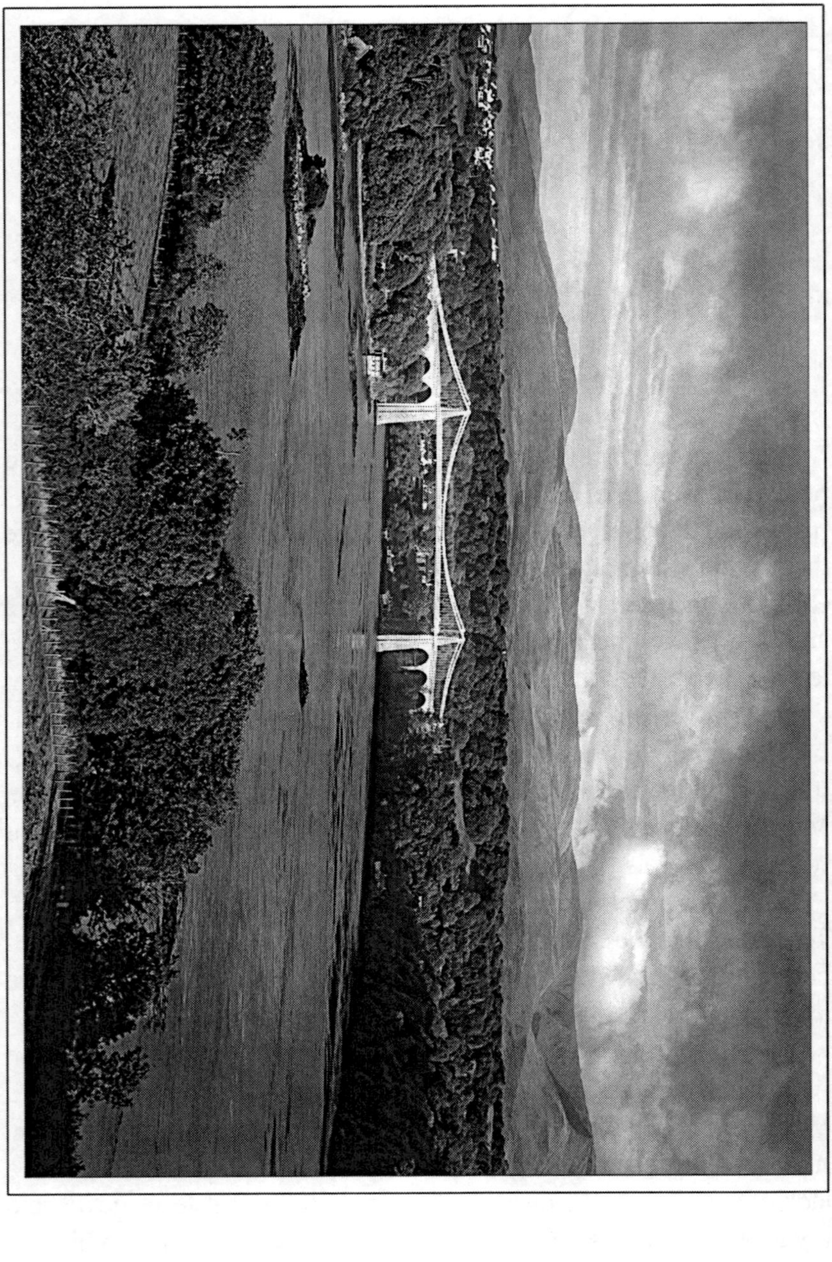

# 28. The Rich Man and Lazarus

"There was a rich man who was dressed in purple and fine linen and lived in luxury every day. At his gate was laid a beggar named Lazarus, covered in sores and longing to eat what fell from the rich man's table. Even the dogs came and licked his sores.

"The time came when the beggar died and the angels carried him to Abraham's side. The rich man also died and was buried. In hell, where he was in torment, he looked up and saw Abraham far away, with Lazarus by his side. So he called to him, 'Father Abraham, have pity on me and send Lazarus to dip the tip of his finger in water and cool my tongue, because I am in agony in this fire.'

"But Abraham replied, 'Son, remember that in your lifetime you received your good things, while Lazarus received bad things, but now he is comforted here and you are in agony. And besides all this, between us and you a great chasm has been fixed, so that those who want to go from here to you cannot, nor can anyone cross over from there to us.'

"He answered, 'Then I beg you, father, send Lazarus to my father's house, for I have five brothers. Let him warn them, so that they will not also come to this place of torment.'

"Abraham replied, 'They have Moses and the Prophets; let them listen to them.'

"'No, father Abraham,' he said, 'but if someone from the dead goes to them, they will repent.'

"He said to him, 'If they do not listen to Moses and the Prophets, they will not be convinced even if someone rises from the dead.' (Luke 16: v. 19–31).

This is a marvellous story, don't you think, full of humour and power. Jesus really stokes the fires to draw the picture and emphasise the contrast. There's even a bit at the end about the stubbornness of unbelief – if we don't want to know, we won't hear the message.

But can he really mean it? Do the rich really deserve to get sent down just because they are rich? The rich man did nothing wrong according to the story. At least, Lazarus was allowed to stay there every day. What would you do if a scruffy tramp was littering the bottom of your drive? You would ring the police and have him (or her) moved on. Perhaps they would find him a place in a hostel.

Then why should Lazarus get the red-carpet treatment in heaven just because he was a poor disabled beggar down here? Obviously, everyone feels sorry for him if he was disabled but it doesn't qualify him for heaven. Surely, he could have done more for himself. Perhaps his folks could have found him a place in a sheltered workshop or something – anything rather than begging.

Well, we are not told whether the rich man had been evil and Lazarus good in order to merit their ultimate destinies, because this is a story about the great reversal rather than about salvation. There is clearly a lot more involved in getting to heaven than our wealth.

But Jesus considered it important enough to tell this powerful and uncomfortable story and we can't escape its implications, however much we water it down. If we spend this life getting and keeping, while stepping over the poor, we shall spend the next wishing we hadn't.

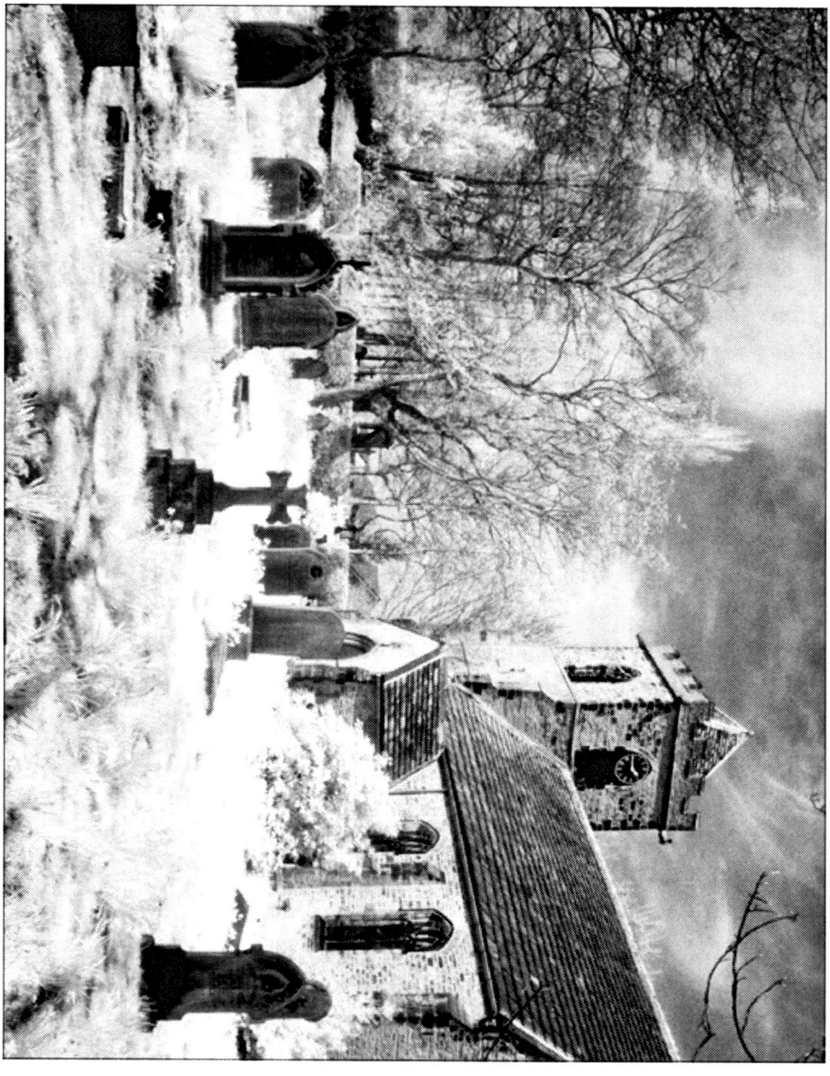

# Epilogue

Have you ever noticed that it was Judas, the betrayer, who looked after the money for Jesus and his disciples? It might have been a coincidence of course, but John didn't think so. According to him – see John 12: v. 6 – Judas had his hands in the till and so John calls him a thief in this acrimonious little verse.

Whatever had gone wrong since that exciting day when Judas had been called by Jesus to join the band of disciples? Surely, Jesus didn't choose Judas because he needed one bad apple for the drama at the end. Nor did he choose Judas to look after the money in order trap him in a temptation he couldn't resist. No, Judas was one with the others. He, too, had left everything to follow Jesus. He was no thief when it all began. Also, he must have been the best man for the cashier's job when the duties were given out but by the time the last chapters were unfolding it had all gone horribly wrong.

Perhaps they had been more successful at raising money than Judas could ever have hoped and, perhaps, an excess of cash was a new and tempting experience for him. But, even so, how could he get it wrong when his days were spent in the blissful presence of Jesus; under his warm but discerning gaze; and, no doubt at times, walking arm in arm?

The answer is money. If it could steal his heart, rob him of his devotion and even cost him his life when he was living in the daily company of Jesus, what do you think it can do to us?

Jesus said, "Everyone who hears these words of mine and puts them into practice is like a wise man who built his house on the rock" (Matthew 7 v. 24).